MANPOWER PLANNING IN A FREE SOCIETY

A Joint Project of the
Industrial Relations Section
Princeton University
and the
Program on Unemployment and the American Economy
of the
Institute of Industrial Relations of the
University of California (Berkeley)

MANPOWER PLANNING IN A FREE SOCIETY

Richard A. Lester

PRINCETON UNIVERSITY PRESS

PRINCETON, NEW JERSEY

1966

Foreword

AT THE END of World War II the major concern in the field of labor economics was union-management relations. Studies of collective bargaining and national labor relations policy occupied the center of the stage. The great policy debates were concerned with whether or not large corporations and nation-wide unions could reach some sort of effective accommodation. The issues of government intervention in labor disputes and government regulation of management and union power commanded most of the attention of labor economists and government practitioners. At this time labor relations seemed to be the core of industrial relations. These concerns and issues, of course, are still important and are still widely discussed.

Today, the spotlight has shifted to another area which, while it always occupied a legitimate place in the field of industrial relations, tended until recently to be neglected. This area of renewed interest is manpower policy. Labor economists are now expressing mounting interest in the development and effective utilization of human resources. The persistence of unemployment in a highly prosperous economy is a matter of grave concern. Investments in man and his development through education are subjects for intensive analysis. Economists see new and exciting problems for study in fields such as vocational education and on-the-job training—which

until a few years ago they had completely over-
looked. And finally, there is fresh new interest in
that overburdened, understaffed, widely maligned,
but critically important organization known as the
Employment Service.

In this volume, Professor Lester throws new light
on old problems and, as he says, sets forth a pattern
of thought and a program of action in some major
areas of manpower policy. His central theme is that
the hand of government can and should be used
more constructively to facilitate effective utilization
of manpower. The role of government should not be
to control or direct manpower, but rather to make
it easier for individuals to choose careers, to prepare
themselves adequately, and to change jobs. This
calls for major improvements in the Employment
Service, a new program of vocational instruction
for school children, more realistic hiring standards
by employers, more informed mobility of labor both
geographically and occupationally, and much greater
stress on knowledge-generating research and distribution of information about manpower needs and
opportunities.

This "think piece," as Professor Lester calls it, presents quite specific and concrete proposals for action. The policy recommendations are based upon
the author's twenty-five years of active experience
and research in the manpower field in the United
States as well as upon a more recent analysis of relevant experience in Western European countries. They
do not call for sweeping new organizations and

institutions; rather they demonstrate how the existing ones may be energized to perform both old and new tasks more effectively in a free-choice society.

This book will have a special interest for professional personnel in the State employment offices throughout the country as well as for those concerned with manpower policy development at the federal level. It should also be particularly useful for labor economists and other members of the academic community engaged in teaching courses on manpower problems and human resource development. And finally, we hope that its concrete proposals for action will command the attention of both State and federal legislators.

FREDERICK HARBISON
Director
Industrial Relations Section

Princeton, New Jersey
December 1, 1965

Preface

THIS BOOK is a combination "think piece" and action program. It presents an approach to the nation's manpower problems and suggests some practical steps to help solve them.

In recent years, considerable progress has been made in the analysis of manpower problems and in the development of practical solutions to them. This book seeks to build on that progress. It analyzes the need for manpower planning, the nature of such planning, and the ways that it could improve the functioning of our mixed economy. Special stress is placed on the proper role of the Federal-State Employment Service in a program for the effective use of the nation's labor resources.

The program proposed in these pages draws heavily on the experience of European democracies, particularly Great Britain, West Germany, and Sweden. The recommendations are, however, definitely focussed on conditions in this country and assume no basic change in our economy or structure of government. For the most part, the suggested actions by government are those that would be appropriate for the Congress and the Administration to take under Title I of the Manpower Development and Training Act (reproduced in the Appendix).

In writing this little volume I have drawn on twenty-five years of experience and research in the manpower field, extending back to employment with four different agencies in World War II. It includes ten years as chairman of the New Jersey Employment Security Council and visits to ten State headquarters in various parts of the country in 1960 in connection with a study of unemployment compensation.

In special preparation for this book, much time has been spent examining employment offices and interviewing practitioners. Since early in 1964 I have visited fifteen local employment offices and State headquarters in four States. During the Spring Term of 1965 spent in Europe on a McCosh Fellowship from Princeton University, I talked with over 100 public officials, employers, labor leaders, and university scholars about the manpower programs in Great Britain, West Germany, and Sweden.

Obviously, persons who have aided in one way or another in the development of this book are too numerous to mention. I should, however, like especially to acknowledge the valuable help I received in this country from Jerome R. Sehulster, State Supervisor of the New Jersey Employment Service, Jack B. Brown, Executive Director of the Pennsylvania Bureau of Employment Security, and Alfred L. Green, Executive Director of the New York Division of Employment; in Great Britain from Thomas Byrne, U.S. Labor Attaché in London and Frank Pickford, Undersecretary in the British Ministry of Labour; in Germany from Vidkunn Ulricksson, U.S. Labor Attaché in Bonn, and Dr. Harry Meisel, head of public relations at the Bundesanstalt für Arbeitsvermittlung und Arbeitslosenversicherung; and in Sweden from Nils Kellgren and Gunnar Olsson of the National Labor Market Board and Arne S. Runske of the Swedish Institute for Cultural Relations. Also, I enjoyed an opportunity to work through and organize my European material at the Rockefeller Foundation's Villa Serbelloni at Bellagio, Italy.

As chairman of the Subcommittee on Research of the National Manpower Advisory Committee, I have benefitted greatly from discussions in the meetings of the Subcommittee and from presentations by staff personnel from the departments of Labor and Health, Education, and Welfare.

Financial and other types of support were provided me by the research project on Unemployment and the American Economy, administered by the University of California at Berkeley under a Ford Foundation grant.

The staff of the Industrial Relations Section of Princeton University has been of assistance in a variety of ways, including preparation of the manuscript for the press.

RICHARD A. LESTER

Princeton, New Jersey
September 1965

Contents

CONTENTS

MANPOWER PLANNING IN A FREE SOCIETY

CHAPTER 1

An Approach to Manpower Problems

THIS BOOK deals with the use of human resources. Its subject matter ranges from the philosophy and economics of manpower planning to proposals for effective administration of particular aspects of a comprehensive program. Most of the ideas presented in these pages can be applied under diverse institutional and economic conditions.

Although its conceptual framework has broad applicability, the book is aimed primarily at improving manpower planning, policy, and operations in the United States. Therefore, it sets forth a pattern of thought and a program of action designed to accomplish the purposes of Title I of the Manpower Development and Training Act of 1962.[1]

The key concepts and recommendations in the book can be applied to America's manpower problems without any basic change in the existing institutional structure or any interference with individual freedoms. In fact, adoption of the recommended program would expand personal liberty by enlarging employment opportunities for individuals.

The manpower experience of European democracies can be instructive for an American program. During the past decade, they generally have had wide-

[1] The language of Title I as amended is presented in the Appendix.

[3]

spread labor shortage, but some localities have suffered from significant unemployment. References to certain policies and results in countries such as Great Britain, West Germany, and Sweden are primarily for purposes of showing the practicality and limitations of particular proposals. Careful examination of foreign manpower programs convinces one that none is, in toto, well suited for the American scene. Nevertheless, manpower policies and measures that have proved successful elsewhere can, with appropriate modification, be part of a consistent program that fits American political and economic structures and employment practices.

Private and Public Manpower Planning

Opinion in the United States about economic planning continues to be somewhat ambivalent. Short-range and long-range planning of their economic affairs by individuals and firms is lauded. However, economic planning by the national government is still somewhat suspect. The national budget, of course, sets forth a plan of expenditure for the ensuing fiscal year. But longer-range and more comprehensive economic planning by the central government is another matter. It raises fears of centralization, bureaucratic domination, and industrial regimentation.

It is unfortunate that the connotations of words often becloud our thinking. Planning as such should not be condemned because of abuses that have been committed in its name. Essentially, it is a process of thinking ahead, a method for anticipating difficulties and seeking, through reasoned action based on fore-knowledge, to guide the course of developments to-ward desired goals. Planning approaches the future with the aid of systematic analysis, so as to minim-ize surprise and uncertainty and to eliminate mis-takes and waste.

Manpower planning applies the process to the preparation and employment of human resources for productive purposes. In a free society, manpower planning aims to enlarge job opportunities and im-prove training and employment decisions, through the power of informed personal choice and calcu-lated adjustment to rapidly changing demand. By means of more intelligent training and career deci-sions and greater adaptability of the nation's labor force, manpower planning can enhance satisfaction on the job, raise the quality and utilization of labor resources, reduce the cost of job search and industry staffing, and, thereby, increase the output of the na-tion.

Properly conceived, manpower planning in our type of economy works with market forces. It does not seek to restrict individual choice or to displace market processes. Rather it enlarges choice and helps the market to operate more effectively by anticipat-ing and arranging for early corrective measures to avoid serious manpower imbalances (restrictive shortages and wasteful surpluses, especially of high-level manpower). Armed with the best obtainable in-formation about future needs for trained manpower of various types, the individuals, firms, and govern-ment agencies can make their plans with respect to

training, location, and work careers more intelligently. Many professions and highly skilled occupations
require five to ten years from the time a young person decides to enter a particular line of work until
he or she has completed all of its educational and
practical requirements. Especially for occupations
with such long lead time, shifts in demand may cause
marked lags in supply and serious labor bottlenecks
unless supply adjustments are facilitated by such
means as proper career information and guidance in
the schools and employment offices, expansion in the
public and private training resources, and the provision for financial and other incentives to enter that
kind of career. Other planned adjustments might include (a) greater breadth of education, combined
with acceleration of specialized training, so that parts
of the work force can be prepared for advanced occupations in a short span of time, and (b) adapta-
tions in demand requirements to permit, for instance,
extensive use of quickly trained assistants. Thus,
basically manpower planning aids in the intelligent
preparation, allocation, and utilization of human resources in our economy.[2]

The Essence of Manpower Planning

Since manpower planning is based on the application of foresight, the first step in any planning program is the development of research so as to improve
the forecasting, by skill categories, of demand and

[2] Technically speaking, such planning helps each worker of
hand and brain to obtain employment in line with his greatest
"comparative advantage."

supply for the nation and for particular industries and areas over, say, the next decade. Such projections can be in terms of rough magnitudes and relative changes or trends. It is, however, desirable to make quite explicit the assumptions on which the projections rest, for purposes of their later revision and of improvement in the methods of manpower forecasting.

The next step is for a central agency to communicate in useable form the content and implications of the forecasts for application by individuals and by agencies that influence career and employment decisions. Such groups include teachers, vocational guidance counselors, educational and training authorities, Employment Service personnel, private employment agencies, company managements, unions, and other governmental and community leaders. In that way individual, company, and governmental plans can be based on the best available information; individuals can be counseled to enter shortage occupations if tests show they have the necessary aptitudes; and company managements can adjust their capital investment, training, and manning plans in the light of such information.

Especially it is important that public and private educational and training programs for youths and adults be guided by information concerning prospective demand and supply for particular professions and occupations. Government-sponsored vocational training programs obviously need to be expanded in areas of prospective shortage, especially if the projected gap is a long-range one, and to be curtailed in lines likely to be seriously overcrowded.

Aware of the relative magnitudes of occupational imbalances, the Employment Service personnel can guide clients and refer them for training and for employment in accordance with the future manpower needs of the economy. It may be important for the employment offices to facilitate particular kinds of labor mobility, to make special efforts to encourage shifts, say, from blue-collar to white-collar work, and to discourage labor mobility that would only complicate manpower imbalances.

To aid labor mobility in the proper directions, managements and unions may need to alter employment practices and compensation structures so as to encourage movement into expanding areas and shortage occupations. In branches of the economy long subject to labor agreements, it is too much to expect that market forces, unaided and expeditiously, could bring about the necessary loosening of worker attachment to particular occupations and could adjust relative wage and benefit levels in line with the nation's manpower needs. Such alterations may be facilitated if they are part of a comprehensive program of manpower planning, stimulated by consideration of the implications that the forecasts have for particular industries and firms.

The actions that workers, businessmen, and governments adopt on the basis of the manpower forecasts do, of course, cause obsolescence in the forecasts themselves. As public and private steps are taken to overcome prospective imbalances in manpower demands and supplies, some of the assumptions on which the occupational, industrial, and geographical projections were made are no longer valid. Therefore, new or revised forecasts must be made periodically. For that purpose, the planning center needs a feedback, so that it can maintain a running inventory of manpower information, classified in meaningful skill categories. Thus, manpower planning is a rather continuous, circular process. The more successful the actions it induces the private and public sectors of the economy to take as a means of meeting projected manpower gaps, the more need there is to revise the forecasts.

Manpower planning does not, however, rest on sands as shifting as these remarks may seem to imply. Continued alteration in supply through career choices occurs only slowly and requires much time because it involves change in conventional views and in the rankings of occupations in popular esteem as well as shifts in training and educational programs. It should be borne in mind that significant expansion in training capacity may mean only small yearly additions to total supply in that occupation. For example, doubling the training capacity for a profession with an average working life of 30 to 35 years may result merely in an annual addition in supply of 3 per cent, assuming that prior thereto the training facilities were just meeting a total replacement need of 3 per cent of supply. Thus, substantial changes in the stock of highly trained manpower in a specialty may require 10 to 15 years to accomplish. Futhermore, substitution of less-trained manpower and use of other techniques for conserving scarce types of supply are, in aggregate, likely to be rather gradual. Consequently, there are not apt to be changes of great magnitude or of direction from, say, one annual forecast to another.

The series of developments outlined in this section gives an idealized version of manpower planning. In practical operation, and even in theoretical analysis, many difficulties confront such a program. Much of this book deals with approaches and policies for overcoming those difficulties. As explained in the next chapter, one of the problems is how manpower planning can effectively operate in a democratic society where it must work through individuals, firms, and the market mechanism and involves the coordinated efforts of various agencies and levels of government.

A Profile of Major Manpower Problems

In a number of respects, the manpower problems facing the United States are more complex and formidable than those confronting Western European countries. America's manpower problems over the next decade promise to be difficult to solve partly because of the nature of projected changes in the labor force, partly because of the level of unemployment and its uneven distribution in our economy, partly because of the combination of rapid shifts in types of employment and increasing barriers to labor mobility, and partly because of the complications of this country's size and its Federal-State-local political structure. Comparisons with other countries may help to bring out the significance of those four features and to illustrate the need for manpower planning in the United States.

1. During the next decade, the working population in the United States is expected to increase at a rate over four times as great as the rate of increase in Great Britain, France, or Sweden, or for the six countries in the European Economic Community taken as a group.[3] Labor-force projections for the United States show an accelerating rate of growth from 1965 to 1975, whereas a decline in the rate of increase is forecast for countries like Great Britain and Sweden and an absolute decline in yearly additions to the labor force for West Germany. The post-war baby boom is responsible for this acceleration in the rate of growth of America's labor force. Between 1965 and 1970 the working population in the United States is expected to grow by 7.5 million, which is an increase 50 per cent greater than occurred from 1960 to 1965.

Furthermore, the largest labor-force increases will be in categories that experience especially high rates of unemployment. Of the 7.5 million total increase between 1965 and 1970, youths from 18 to 24 years of age and Negroes will constitute a disproportionately large share. In that period, the annual waves of new young workers will swell the number of 18-to-24-year-

[3] See *The Pattern of the Future*, Manpower Studies No. 1, Ministry of Labour, Her Majesty's Stationery Office, London, 1964, p. 8.

old work-seekers by more than 3 million. In the same five years, the nonwhites in the labor force will expand by almost a million and a half, nearly twice their increase during the preceding five years.

The growing additions of youths and nonwhites to the labor force threaten to aggravate the nation's unemployment problem. Older teenagers and young people in their early twenties have the highest unemployment rates of any age group. From 1960 through 1965, the unemployment rate for white males averaged 12 and 13 per cent for the 18-and-19-year-old group and 7 and 8 per cent for 20-24-year-olds. For nonwhite workers of all ages the annual unemployment rates for that five-year period were between 10 and 12 per cent; for nonwhites 18 and 19 years of age they ranged from 22 to 27 per cent. Generally, nonwhite workers have been twice as likely to be unemployed as white workers.

2. In recent years, the matching of total labor demand and total labor supply has been much more successful in European democracies and in Japan than in the United States. The consequence has been that general labor shortage rather than unemployment has been an acute problem in those countries. That has been true despite inflows of large numbers of workers from other countries into West Germany, Sweden, and Great Britain.

During the six years ending with 1964, unemployment rates in Great Britain, France, West Germany, Sweden, and Japan were but one-quarter to one-half as high, measured on a comparable basis, as the unemployment rates for the United States.[4] In view of the labor-supply projections and the amounts of imported labor in particular countries, the prospect is for a continuation of some such differentials in unemployment rates between those countries and the United States, at least for the next few years.

Various explanations have been offered for the marked differences in unemployment rates between the United States and the other countries during the 1959-64 period. Doubtless one factor has been the greater pressure of aggregate demand on aggregate supply in the low-unemployment nations. That pressure is reflected in price-level changes. During that same six-year period, the rate of increase in consumer prices in the European countries and Japan was two to five times as rapid as in the United States.

Without doubt another significant factor in the unemployment differences has been the more systematic arrangements for transition from school to work in Great Britain, West Germany, Sweden, and other European countries. As explained more fully in Chapter 3, career study in school, vocational counseling for high school students, and formal apprenticeship play a much more important role in those countries than they do in the United States. For example, of 304,000 boys entering employment in 1963 in Great Britain, one-third or 102,000 were apprenticed to skilled occupations; in the same year in the United

[4] See A. F. Neff, "International Unemployment Rates," *Monthly Labor Review*, 88 (March 1965), p. 258.

States, with a labor force three times the size of Great Britain's, the total of newly registered apprentices was only 57,204. Germany in 1963 had a total of 1,194,000 apprentice contracts; the figure for the United States was only one-tenth of that.[5]

The rate of unemployment among youths in Great Britain, West Germany, and Sweden has, generally speaking, been no greater than among adults. Actually, from 1952 to 1965 the rate of unemployment among males under 18 in Great Britain has each year been below the rate for all males.[6] In contrast, the annual rate of unemployment among 16- and 17-year-old male workers in the United States has been about three times the rate for all male workers each year from 1947 to 1965, and the rate for males 20-24 has consistently been almost twice as high.[7] The postwar baby boom and relatively high unemployment since 1957 in this country can hardly explain differentials of that size extending over such a long period.

[5] For a discussion of apprenticeship in the United States and in Great Britain, Western Germany, and France see *The Role of Apprenticeship in Manpower Development: United States and Western Europe*, Vol. 3 of *Selected Readings in Employment and Manpower*, Subcommittee on Employment and Manpower, Committee on Labor and Public Welfare, U.S. Senate, 88th Congress, 2nd Session, U.S. Government Printing Office, Washington, D.C., 1964, especially pp. 1275-1357.

[6] *Ibid.*, pp. 1296-1297 supplemented by calculations for 1964 and 1965.

[7] Figures for the United States are in the *Manpower Report of the President . . . 1965*, U.S. Government Printing Office, Washington, D.C., 1965, pp. 204-205.

3. Great shifts have occurred in the composition of labor demand and in America's labor force during the past decade, and they promise to continue over the next decade, perhaps at an accelerated pace. Because those broad shifts require significant adjustments in occupations and career patterns, in education and vocational training, in workers' geographical location, and in employer practices, manpower planning will be more important and more needed in the future than in the past.

The United States is the first country to experience a pronounced shift in employment from goods manufacture to a predominantly service-supplying economy. In part that shift is the result of the increased demand for services like education, medical care, recreation, and finance that comes with higher income levels, and in part it is the consequence of the declining demand for physical labor that stems from automation and other labor-saving advances in industry.[8] Accompanying the shift has been a marked expansion in white-collar employment, a levelling off of blue-collar employment, and a pronounced absolute decline in farm employment. Furthermore, the adjustment in the nation's labor force required with the shift from goods production to service industries has been

[8] The rate of technological advance between 1954 and 1964 seems to have been at least as rapid in European countries like Great Britain, West Germany, and Sweden as in the United States. Although those countries may have started from a less advanced base, their rate of increase in productivity (output per man hour) appears to have been even greater than in the American economy during that decade.

complicated by two factors: (a) the high wage-benefit levels in most goods production except agriculture and some soft goods, and the low wage-benefit levels in most service lines, and (b) worker ties to particular firms because of seniority, company benefits, and other employer practices and employee protections.

A somewhat more detailed discussion of these employment shifts and barriers to labor mobility may help to show their implications for manpower planning. Mere statistics are dull, but examination of trends is thought-provoking and leads to speculation about causes and remedies. This discussion of employment shifts and obstacles to labor mobility does not, however, imply any judgment as to the extent that deficient demand or structural difficulties are responsible for the total volume of unemployment in the United States.

Beginning in 1953, the number of workers in industries making goods began to decline in absolute amounts. From 1953 to 1963, total employment in goods production is estimated to have declined from 33.3 million to 31.4 million.[9] The proportion of the nation's employment in goods-producing industries fell below 50 per cent in 1955, was 45 per cent in 1963, and will continue to decline in the future.

In the service industries, employment doubled from

[9] The figures in this and the next paragraph have been taken from V. R. Fuchs, "Some Implications of the Growing Importance of the Service Industries," in *The Task of Economics*, Forty-Fifth Annual Report, National Bureau of Economic Research, Inc., New York, 1965, pp. 6-8.

1929 to 1963, rising from 18.6 million to 38 million. In that period employment in the service industries (including personal, professional, financial, and governmental services, and repair service and trade) rose from 40 per cent to 55 per cent of the nation's total employment. In 1956, the number of white-collar workers surpassed the total of blue-collar workers and by 1964, with 31 million white-collar workers (professional, technical, managerial, clerical, sales, and kindred workers), accounted for 44 per cent of the nation's labor force compared with 36 per cent for blue-collar workers. During the same eight years, farm workers declined by 2 million, falling from 10 per cent to 6.3 per cent of the country's labor force.[10] Farm workers displaced from agriculture have special problems of adjustment to factory and white-collar employment.

In terms of work forces and wage-benefit levels, important differences exist between goods production and service lines. In goods production, four-fifths of the employees are males, displacement of labor by technological change is common, increases in labor productivity generally are high, and seasonal unemployment is especially prevalent in certain lines such as clothing, toys, and canning. In the service industries, women hold nearly half the jobs, a high percentage of the workers are part-time employees and self-employed, employment is generally more stable, and union-management agreements are less likely to con-

[10] Service workers, including those in private households, account for the remaining 13.2 per cent.

trol the terms and conditions of employment and thus to encourage strong company ties and barriers to labor mobility.

With respect to wage-benefit levels for comparable work, goods-production lines that are highly unionized and highly mechanized such as auto, aircraft, metals, machinery, and rubber, and less-well-organized industries such as petroleum and chemicals, are high-wage and high-benefit industries. On the other hand, service lines, except for transportation, are generally low in wage and benefit levels. The wage level is low in government service, hospitals, schools, banks and insurance companies, retail trade, hotels and restaurants, and for service in and around the home, and company-financed benefits are relatively low except in the case of banks and insurance. Data are not available for determining exact differences in combined wage-benefit levels as between industries or groups of industries. On a strictly comparable basis, perhaps service industries as a group would have a wage level at least 10 per cent below that for goods-producing industries as a group. The differential in terms of company benefits would average much more than 10 per cent.

Such wage and benefit differentials present an obstacle to the movement of workers from contracting goods-producing industries to expanding service lines. Additional barriers take the form of seniority in lay-off and promotion rights, benefits graded by seniority (e.g., vacations and pensions), and loss of benefit rights with interfirm transfer. Generally speaking, wage-level differences between goods and service lines seem somewhat smaller in percentage terms in European countries such as Great Britain, West Germany, and Sweden. And in those countries, seniority is less controlling and benefits are less a barrier to interfirm and interindustry movement of labor because government schemes provide a much higher proportion of all employee benefits than is the case in the United States.

4. Manpower problems in the United States are complicated by the size and diversity of the country and by a scattering of manpower responsibilities among agencies in four different levels of government—Federal, State, Municipal, and School District.

In countries the size of Sweden (working population 4,700,000), or West Germany (working population 27,000,000), or Great Britain (working population 25,000,000), it is easier to visualize the economy and the work force and to achieve unity of purpose, standards, and programs in the manpower field. The United States is a continent, with great diversity in employment conditions, in racial and nationality groupings, in the educational background of different elements in the labor force, and in attitudes about employment and governmental policy. Geographical mobility is high compared with European countries. For many occupations the market is essentially nationwide or continental, but for other occupations the market is strictly local, and for some others it is no more than regional.

AN APPROACH TO MANPOWER PROBLEMS

In the United States, manpower functions and policy-making are rather decentralized and are scattered among such a variety of agencies as to make coordination a serious problem. Public education, most vocational education, and most career counseling activities are under the authority of State departments of education and local school boards. However, the Federal Government enters into training under the Manpower Development and Training Act of 1962 and the Economic Opportunity Act of 1964, and the Federal-State Employment Service and the Veterans' Administration are engaged in career counseling. Although it is Federally financed, the public Employment Service consists of fifty separate agencies, each with its own State pay scale, each with a completely independent staff, and each with a separate budget and its own program. Furthermore, private fee-charging employment agencies are engaged in the placement and counseling of workers, and they have twice as many local offices and a staff total at least as large as the Federal-State Employment Service.[11] Although the State Employment Services only account for an estimated 16 per cent of all new hires, attempts to improve their effectiveness since 1960 have been met with charges that the Em-

[11] See L. P. Adams, "Private Employment Agencies" in *Readings on Public Employment Services*, compiled for the Select Subcommittee on Labor, Committee on Education and Labor, House of Representatives, 88th Congress, 2nd Session, December 1964, U.S. Government Printing Office, Washington, D.C., 1965, p. 757.

ployment Service aims to "gain control of the placement market" and is engaged in a "great manpower
grab."[12]

In Germany, referral of workers and apprentices
for placement and also all vocational counseling may,
by law, be performed only by the Federal Institute
of Labor Placement and Unemployment Insurance
or agencies designated by it. The Institute, a self-man-
aging corporation, has eleven State (Länder) units,
but they are an integral part of the national program
of the Institute.

In Sweden, the National Labor Market Board has
supervision of the public Employment Service and
control of all private employment agencies, employs
or partly employs all vocational counselors, helps to
finance and run adult training programs, influences
the allocation of emergency public works, licenses
the starting permits for building construction, and
engages in a number of other manpower-affecting
activities. To a considerable extent, the National
Board, a semi-independent unit, delegates its functions to twenty-five County Labor Market Boards
(Länsarbetsnämnd). Clearly, manpower planning
and programs in Germany and especially in Sweden
are much more unified and coordinated than in the
United States. Great Britain, however, suffers almost
as much as the United States from divided authority

[12] See, for example, "Big Government Jumps Into the Job-
Hunting Field," *Standard Oiler*, employee magazine of the
Standard Oil Company of California, June 1963; and Frank T.
Bow, "The Great Manpower Grab," *Reader's Digest*, Octo-
ber 1964.

and uncoordinated activity in the manpower field.

Inadequate coordination of manpower policy and programs, poor interstate communication and placement, and low average quality of State Employment Service personnel are serious problems for manpower planning and operations in the United States. They can, however, be reduced and solved without abandoning either decentralization of operations or local experimentation and the adaptation of national policies to local conditions.

In succeeding chapters, measures are proposed to help solve aspects of the four major manpower problems discussed above. The proposals include ways to facilitate the transition from school to work, to improve the interstate matching of men and jobs and reduce barriers to mobility, to raise the quality of the staff of the Employment Service, and to increase the coordination of various manpower activities in this country. The next chapter provides the analytical background for examination in succeeding chapters of various aspects of manpower problems, manpower planning, and manpower operations and staff.

■■

CHAPTER 2

Manpower Planning and the Market

■■

THE idealized version of manpower planning outlined in the preceding chapter clearly assumes widespread use of well-founded, official information on which to base programs of vocational counseling, education and training, and company staffing. This chapter carries that discussion forward, with application particularly to career and employment choices. It considers the problems of career planning and aids to rational vocational choices. Since manpower planning seeks to improve career development and labor mobility, the bases for deciding what is desirable and what is undesirable mobility are examined. Then consideration is given to the role of market criteria as a means for obtaining the proper mobility and allocation of labor in the economy. The chapter ends with a discussion of the ways by which, through manpower planning activities, the market indicators can be made more effective for mobility and allocation purposes.

The Problems of Career Planning

The youngster or adult who seeks to make the most rational choice of career is faced nowadays with many obstacles and uncertainties. The world of employment has become increasingly large, complex, and specialized. Compensation is not just money but a bundle of benefit rights, employee privileges, and job protections. Rational choice of a career involves not only long-range forecasting of demand and supply for particular occupations and industries but also weighing such incommensurables as nonmonetary forms of compensation, promotion possibilities, and the likelihood of the elimination of part or all of one's investment in training for an occupation because of technological advance. In an economy characterized by rapid change, it will be common for workers to have to start in a new occupation or industry on two or more occasions during their lifetimes.

Faced with the task of assessing his own abilities for a wide range of career possibilities, the youngster usually lacks adequate data on different careers, expert neutral guidance in career selection, and information about training in terms of quality, time, and personal expense. It is readily recognized that a person with a physical handicap, mental deficiency, or psychological quirk needs guidance in preparation for the world of work and during the early period of his employment. It should be equally evident that persons hampered by ignorance, by weakness in self-appraisal, or by lack of skill in job search are also handicapped and need guidance. Many entrants into the labor force suffer from shortcomings in their environment. Their parents, teachers, and community leaders may have quite limited career horizons; that is especially likely to be the case in one-industry towns and in rural areas. Proper training facilities for all but a few occupations may also be lacking in such communities.

The next chapter considers in detail the desirable organization, content, and quality of vocational counseling under manpower planning in the United States. Here it is sufficient to point out the need for such guidance and to note that neither the schools nor market forces can be expected to meet that need. As the next chapter explains, certain European countries have extensive programs of career information and analysis in the public schools. They spend as much class time on education for intelligent career selection as some of our high schools do in a term of "drivers education." We have something to learn from them with respect to the relative significance of different subjects in the high school curriculum. Those countries have also found it advantageous to give a central agency the responsibility for preparing material and providing the leadership for vocational guidance activity.

Company Planning and Desirable Mobility

In the United States, large firms have for many years engaged in manpower planning for the higher executive categories. Commonly the programs have been known as "executive development." They have involved special arrangements for training and breadth of experience for employees who have high executive potential.

More recently, similar programs of recruitment,

training, and development have been instituted for engineers and other professional groups in the business corporation. These programs also involve planning individual careers for company personnel.

Shortages of certain skilled employees and the use of computers for staff planning have stimulated the application of projection and analytical techniques to lower levels of manpower within companies in the United States and Europe. For example, analysis of attrition or survival rates of employees in different departments over past periods provides a basis for estimating the company's manpower needs, say, for the next five years. Contrasts in survival rates and in turnover rates raise questions concerning the factors that explain such variation. It is interesting to note that in some industries (for example, steel and electronics in Sweden) which have good research programs and fairly stable production techniques, reliable manpower forecasts can be made for all job categories over a five-year period.

In addition to internal data, such firms obtain information for purposes of manpower planning and recruitment from outside sources. They make comparative studies of labor turnover and wage-benefit levels; they analyze the flow of job applications; they use skill surveys and other data from the public employment offices; they obtain information from private employment agencies and consultants; and they get a "feel for the market" from recruitment visits at colleges and from conversations with vocational school teachers and the flow of employment applications. Company managements wish to recruit from a variety of sources not only for purposes of selection but also to have a better understanding of the manpower situation and future prospects.

Large firms may have less difficulty in personnel planning because they represent distinct and extensive mobility units, and because part of the work force is "locked in" by company ties. The large firm is likely to have its own training program, definite ladders of promotion, and a sufficient range of occupations so that employees can be offered, over a period of time, choices among a variety of jobs. Under the company's personnel program, efforts are made to have employees develop a work career with the company. The worker can accept an entrance job without making definite career plans and, after gaining some experience and knowledge of the company, make a career choice from among the range of occupations represented in the company. On-the-job training and company-financed education stimulate movement into higher positions. Delayed choice may be encouraged in branches such as sales, personnel, and some categories of office work. Studies indicate that it may be easier for a person to shift from blue-collar to white-collar work within a company than it is to make such a shift by moving to another company. One reason may be that company requirements for entrance into certain white-collar jobs are less exacting for persons already well attached to the firm.[1]

[1] See J. L. Stern and D. B. Johnson, "Blue to White Collar Mobility: A Preliminary Report," *Proceedings of the Social*

The industrial relations policies of many companies also tend to restrict interfirm mobility. Movement between firms is penalized under a company policy of hiring into the bottom jobs, promoting largely according to seniority aided by on-the-job training, and varying benefits and vacations according to seniority (length of service with that company). If the employee transfers to another company having the same policy, he must start again in one of its bottom jobs as a probationary employee, at first without any seniority rights for promotion or recall from lay-off, without certain employee benefit and vacation rights, and without the protections of the grievance procedure against arbitrary disciplinary action including dismissal. With such a loss of valuable rights and such handicaps as a new employee in another firm, it is understandable that employees with a few years of seniority tend to be "locked into" that firm.[2] And the great value of seniority in terms of perquisites and priorities explains the pressures that employees and their unions exert for further measures of employee security designed to avoid loss of such rights with rapid change in company employment and in occupational patterns.

The "locked-in" effect produced by tying employee

Statistics Section, 1964, American Statistical Association, Washington, D.C., 1965, pp. 171-172.

[2] See R. A. Lester, *Hiring Practices and Labor Competition*, Industrial Relations Section, Princeton University, 1954, Chapter 5; and L. G. Reynolds, *The Structure of Labor Markets*, Harper and Brothers, New York, 1951, pp. 79-83.

rights to seniority is strengthened by other company policies and practices that hamper interfirm mobility. Companies, through an association or by convention, may follow an anti-pirating code. Under such a code of employment ethics, a firm may hire a job applicant currently employed at another company only if that company's management has no serious objection and the worker gives sufficient advance notice of intention to quit.[3] Also, managements may have a policy of not hiring workers on lay-off from another company because it is fairly certain that, upon recall, such workers would leave and return to their regular employer in order to preserve the valuable rights they had accumulated under seniority. Temporary loans of skilled employees may, however, be arranged by companies following these anti-pirating practices.

Such management policies and practices raise interesting questions concerning the desirable kinds and amounts of labor mobility—questions that must be faced in any program of manpower planning. It is evident that, from the viewpoint of an individual company, most labor turnover occurring after a probationary period is expensive and wasteful. It costs the company a considerable amount in money and resources to recruit, to test and select, to place on the payroll and in a job, and to indoctrinate and train

[3] See Lester, *Hiring Practices and Labor Competition* (see n. 2), pp. 62-65; and Lester, *Adjustments to Labor Shortages*, Industrial Relations Section, Princeton University, 1955, pp. 46-49, for a discussion of the operation of such anti-pirating codes.

a new employee. The firm loses that investment in him if he leaves, which explains why managements are so interested in their labor turnover figures and seek to keep them low.

From a national viewpoint, much labor turnover may also be a waste and have an adverse effect on the Gross National Product. Some interfirm movement of labor may, however, make a net contribution to the economy as a whole. Any temporary loss of company investment in the man that is not transferable may be more than offset by the long-run gain in total productivity. That could be the case under one of the following conditions: (1) if the person qualifies for a higher-level job and the firm where he is presently employed cannot use those talents or skills; (2) if the person's total earnings could be increased over the long run by a shift of employment from one industry or area to another; or (3) if, by means of training, he could be qualified for a higher-level job so that the increase in his total earnings (properly discounted) would exceed the training costs. In each case, of course, account should be taken of the "national loss" or cost of interemployer transfer, with some allowance on the other hand for any gain in the worker's job satisfactions.

Clearly it may be difficult in particular cases to estimate the value of each factor and to try to arrive at a net balance in national terms. Policy decisions may be especially complicated by possible divergence between desirable mobility from the viewpoint of the individual firm and optimum mobility from the national viewpoint, and also by possible differences between the actual short-run and the estimated long-run interest of the individual worker. It is such conceivable differences of interest that cause conflicts of opinion about public policy in the manpower field and that make it so necessary, through careful analysis and research findings, to develop a definition of optimum mobility that a manpower agency can readily apply in actual cases. To illustrate by example, some critics have insisted that the public Employment Service should not register and refer to jobs persons already employed, regardless of any resulting gains in pay and in use of·talents. Actually, the State Employment Services should make many more such referrals than they do. Only an estimated 2 to 3 per cent of the Services' placements in nonagricultural employment have involved moving from one job to another, whereas Bureau of Census survey data indicate that probably about three-fifths of the people hired and rehired in this country each year are employed at the time they change jobs.[4]

The issue of policy is how, under manpower planning, desirable mobility should be promoted and undesirable mobility be discouraged and minimized.[5] Proper career information, testing and vocational

[4] *The Role and Mission of the Federal-State Employment Service in the American Economy*, Committee on Education and Labor, House of Representatives, 88th Congress, 2nd Session, December 1964, U.S. Government Printing Office, Washington, D.C., 1965, pp. 32-33.

[5] Chapter 6 contains a discussion of labor mobility and a proposal for "mobility guidelines."

[31]

counseling, preemployment training, and placement can help to reduce the volume of quits and thus reduce unnecessary turnover. Desirable mobility may be aided by training opportunities that provide workers with a "second chance" to qualify for higher-level employment, or by a good system of interarea job clearance and aid in paying the transfer costs of the individual, which help to equalize employment opportunities for persons with the same talents and training in different areas of the country.

Clearly a public Employment Service cannot be guided simply by employer interest, labor-union interest, or the short-run interest of workers. As a public agency it should consider the long-run national interest as well as the long-range interest of individuals, firms, and the community. A public Employment Service should not make decisions based solely on current pay differences between jobs, without regard to future possibilities, nor should it select employment in a low-level job with no promotion prospects over training that promises good future employment for a man although at a temporary cost to the government and to the man. It is a responsibility of manpower planning, with the aid of research findings, to work out the proper order of priority in such matters.

The Effectiveness of Market Indicators

To be fully effective, manpower planning should operate with and through market forces. The information, counseling, vocational education, and job-referral programs are aimed at improving choices of occupation, use of training resources, and labor mobility. Therefore, they serve to supplement and strengthen the operation of the market mechanism in the labor field.[6]

In a free economy with private ownership of a large part of the productive equipment, main reliance is placed on market indicators to achieve, through individual choices, the rational allocation and economical use of resources. Price, as the chief market indicator, directs consumer and producer demand and serves to allocate the factors of production and their output among competing uses. For the most part consumer demand, which guides production in a free society, consists of individual choices made in the light of present and prospective prices. The demands of government and corporations represent, of course, decisions of collective units.

In the labor field, many decisions are arrived at by collective negotiations. Collective bargaining fixes not only "price" (wages) but also the collective purchase of employee benefits and other perquisites. In the absence of unionization, collective purchase can be said to exist when the company adopts programs such as employee benefits, insurance, and vacations, and insists that employees take a part of their compensation in those exact forms and quantities. However,

[6] Of course, the closer the purchase and sale of labor everywhere approach the conditions of a "perfect market," especially in terms of information and foresight, the less need there would be for manpower planning by government.

collective choice and compulsory purchase do not basically alter the fact that private purchase and sale mean reliance on the market mechanism for decisions concerning the development, allocation, and use of economic resources. Although in the labor field, collective negotiations may fix price (wages, benefits, and other nonpecuniary compensation) for a period of a year or more, employment is still largely governed by market forces.

The effectiveness of market forces in solving manpower problems can best be examined by analyzing different facets of the subject. For that purpose, the discussion will be divided into the following topics: (1) information, (2) counseling and motivation, (3) unemployment, (4) discrimination in employment, (5) adaptability of compensation, (6) elimination of shortages, and (7) areas of greatest effectiveness.

1. The market can hardly be expected to provide expert information for career and job selection to all persons who need it. Nor can the market be presumed to provide the employment and labor-supply information that managements need for well-informed decisions with respect to recruiting, compensating, and training employees. There is no central market or set of market quotations; each employer can almost be considered a separate market. Advertisements in the newspapers are only samples of the available vacancies, and cannot provide an adequate basis for objective comparison and forecasting. A commercial service to provide the necessary information to all

who need it throughout the country would not be feasible. Workers generally would not be in a position to demand and pay for such a service, and the same would be true for many employers. Only a central unit, supported by government, can collect all the necessary data, subject it to analysis and research, and package and distribute the processed information effectively to all parts of society.

2. The private sector of the economy does provide some vocational counseling and strong incentives for occupational advancement. Employee counseling is available and practiced effectively in many large firms. Economic incentives are sufficiently well known to motivate many workers to take training and to strive to climb up the occupational ladder.

The market is, however, weak in supplying most individuals with neutral, test-based advice and guidance in career selection and development. Also, it is not very effective in motivating youths from poorer areas and homes to take proper preemployment training and other measures for occupational improvement. These shortcomings in the market mechanism arise partly from a lack of proper information. Also, the economic incentives may lack effectiveness without expert advice to indicate the possibilities and steps that can lead to occupational advancement. The market tends to emphasize present employment opportunities and pay, often at the expense of long-run personal improvement. The child labor laws are a case in point. They were necessary in order to prevent economic pressures, and parents, from injuring the personal development of children and thereby reducing the potential productivity of the economy.

3. In a sense unemployment continues to exist on a wide scale because the market does not ensure that workers can sell their labor even if they price it quite low. The extent to which unemployment is caused by the unwillingness of society to permit the market mechanism to operate freely and fully in the labor sphere is too complex an issue for treatment here. Clearly part of the unemployment at any one time represents imbalance, because unfilled demand in the form of job vacancies exists and has bottle-neck effects on employment expansion.

Manpower planning can aid the market and can reduce the economic loss from unemployment in at least three ways. Better information and the operation of employment exchanges for the matching of demand and supply can shorten the periods of joblessness that workers experience.[7] Periods of unemployment can be utilized to train and retrain workers so as to improve an individual's subsequent prospects for employment. And employers can be encouraged

[7] See, for example, the statement Paul Little of the California Employment Service made, "Repeated studies of these referral practices in California show the public service is able to cut the elapsed time of job filling substantially, often by several weeks," in *Public Employment Service*, Hearings before the Select Subcommittee on Labor, Committee on Education and Labor, House of Representatives, 88th Congress, 2nd Session, U.S. Government Printing Office, Washington, D.C., 1964, p. 325. Further reference is made to this statement in Chapter 7.

to modify employment practices, and casual work can be organized (e.g., in agriculture and also in service lines as explained in Chapter 5) so as to increase employment in total and especially for less advantaged workers.

4. Before the mid-1960's, the market failed to prevent widespread racial discrimination in employment in both the South and the North. Part of the differential in earnings and employment levels between Negroes and whites was due to differences in education and environment. But part, as studies clearly show, was genuine discrimination—the denial of employment and promotion simply on the basis of color.[8] Such race discrimination, not eliminated by market forces, tended to create a vicious circle of restricted employment opportunities, low-level living, discouragement, limited ambition, and lack of preparation for advanced posts in industry. Action by government against race discrimination in employment and to improve the preparation of Negroes for employment has tended to break this vicious circle. Now in some large firms Negroes actually have preference over whites for certain higher-level jobs. Also, experience has already indicated that better information, training, and counseling are helping to motivate a significant number of Negro youths.

5. Under a price system in a free market economy, the comparative attractiveness of jobs as represented

[8] See R. A. Lester, *Economics of Labor* (2nd ed.) Macmillan, New York, 1964, pp. 531-538, for further discussion on this matter and reference to one of the studies.

by differences in compensation[9] is supposed to cause labor to be distributed among occupations, industries, and areas so as to maximize production and worker satisfaction. In the theory of the market economy, relative compensation serves to direct labor so that, for each skill category, there is an equilibrium between demand and supply in all industries and localities. Compensation differentials are supposed to change in response to shifts in demand for and supply of labor in different skill classes, and labor is assumed to move between employers in response to changes in interfirm, interindustry, and interarea differences in compensation.

Such a labor marketing system can operate effectively only under certain conditions. Workers must have information about all available jobs, including details about their "compensation" and a basis for knowing whether they would qualify and be hired. Employers would need to permit workers to move freely between firms and not seek to obstruct labor turnover by industrial relations policies and practices. Both employers and workers would need to allow relative rates of compensation (differentials between occupations, industries, and areas) to fluctuate freely and directly in response to demand and supply.

It is evident that existing conditions in the United States are far from that market ideal. Companies usually change wages uniformly for all occupations

[9] The term "compensation" includes not only wages but also "fringe benefits" of all kinds and other advantageous conditions of work.

in the company, either in cents per hour or in percentage terms. Only infrequently does a company significantly alter occupational differentials in pay and then not necessarily for labor-supply reasons. The factors favoring stability in occupational wage differentials within a company are usually quite strong, whether the company is unionized or not. Although gradual alterations in interindustry differences in pay may occur, there has for half a century been a remarkable stability in the wage ranking of most industries in a number of countries.[10]

The factors influencing wage changes and those determining employment changes may not be closely connected. Recent studies of correlation between changes in employment and changes in hourly earnings find little consistent relationship between the two over the past ten or fifteen years. Within limits, an increase in employment in an industry or firm is no more likely to be accompanied by a relative increase in earnings than would be true for a decrease in employment in an industry or firm.[11]

[10] See D. E. Cullen, "The Interindustry Wage Structure, 1899-1950," *American Economic Review*, 46 (June 1956), pp. 353-369; and *Wages and Labor Mobility*, Working Party of the Economic Policy Committee, Office of Economic Cooperation and Development, Paris, France, 1965, pp. 22-32.

[11] See Lloyd Ulman, "Labor Mobility and the Industrial Wage Structure in the Postwar United States," *Quarterly Journal of Economics*, 79 (February 1965), pp. 77-94; *Wages and Labour Mobility* (see n. 10), pp. 85-118; E. H. Phelps Brown and M. H. Browne, "Earnings in Industries of the United Kingdom, 1948-59," *Economic Journal*, 72 (September 1962), pp. 534-536 and 544; and Ynge Åberg, "The

Such a lack of correlation appears to lend support to Clark Kerr's conclusion that there are both a set of wage-determining factors (a wage market) and a set of employment-determining factors (a job market), with much less overlap or connection between them than economists have been wont to assume.

6. The lack of a closer relationship between pay and labor supply helps to explain why manpower policy cannot simply rely on changes in compensation to eliminate labor shortages. It must use other influences as well, because appropriate changes in compensation do not occur soon enough and because compensation rates alone are not sufficiently effective to achieve the needed labor mobility.

To help in the expeditious elimination of a particular labor shortage, adjustment in the compensation for that occupation may need to be accompanied by some of the following measures: (a) a program of information and counseling to help individuals appreciate and take advantage of the opportunities in the occupation; (b) an increase in the training facilities in that line; (c) arrangements for accelerated training and refresher courses to shorten periods of

---

Relationship between Wage and Employment Changes in Individual Firms," *The Swedish Journal of Economics*, 67 (June 1965), pp. 101-124. The Åberg study, based on data for individual firms and year-to-year changes, found the relationship between wage and employment change in Sweden to be "extremely weak," even weaker than revealed by some other studies.

preparation; (d) efforts to draw back into the labor force qualified persons with prior experience (e.g., teachers, nurses, secretaries); (e) improvements in transportation, housing, and schools and assistance in meeting transfer costs where those are hampering factors, as they may be if geographical mobility is involved; (f) efforts to change social attitudes toward an occupation where such attitudes limit supply; and (g) a program to encourage wider use of substitute arrangements and to relax worker ties to particular firms.

Stress on nonpecuniary influences in labor supply and demand should not be taken as depreciating the importance of pay in employment and labor mobility. The significance of compensation will, of course, differ in particular cases. Compensation is clearly a real obstacle to a shift of workers from automating factories with high wage-benefit levels into service lines (like education, hospital care, recreation, and retail distribution) with low wage-benefit levels. Unemployed auto workers hesitate to take new jobs with similar requirements in schools, hospitals, hotels, and department stores. However, more than pay and fringe benefits is involved in such reluctance. Men may prefer manipulating machines to serving people, especially if many women in the service lines have the same or higher-level jobs. Social attitudes can be an important factor in labor supply in particular occupations and industries, and it may take more than information and counseling to bring about a marked change in such work attitudes.

[41]

7. Market forces seem to operate most effectively for the professions, for certain self-contained industries, and for graduating seniors in high schools, voçational schools, and colleges and universities. Those in the professions (e.g., doctors, lawyers, nurses, teachers, and physical and social scientists) have their own professional associations. Members of the profession are generally well supplied with information about compensation and employment opportunities, which for any qualified individual may extend over the whole country. Usually professional people have made their occupational choices early in life and remain in the chosen profession throughout their working days. A profession has a common standard of preparation and professional conduct, which establishes a minimum basis of quality for all members.

Certain rather self-contained industries and skilled trades have characteristics similar to the professions. For example, the maritime occupations have their own hiring halls, and, in skilled occupations such as the printing and building trades, the union often serves as an employment exchange.

For graduating students, whether college seniors or girls completing a secretarial course, a rather well-organized market often exists. A new supply becomes available at a particular time, and many firms make offers in advance of that date. Teachers or placement offices serve as information disseminators, counselors, and agents for recruiting firms. In those cases, there may be a closer relationship between starting pay and quality of the worker than is generally true.[12]

In such situations, the need for the public Employment Service to supply information, counseling, and job clearance facilities is not great. Other market institutions and agents perform such services. It is noteworthy that in many countries these sections of the labor force generally have a low rate of use of the public Employment Service, often despite vigorous efforts to draw them in. In some cases, the public Service has completely taken over the job exchange function for a profession or industry in a city or a State.

In some respects, large firms resemble self-contained industries with respect to manpower. Market forces may operate somewhat effectively at the "ports of entry" (the hiring-in jobs) but exert much less influence on compensation for and mobility to jobs filled by promotion from within. It is somewhat questionable, therefore, to refer to manpower developments within the corporation as the operations of an "internal market." Rather they represent administered wages and benefits and administered occupational advance under semi-monopolistic conditions.

[12] See G. P. Shultz, "A Nonunion Market for White Collar Labor" and "Comments," in *Aspects of Labor Economics,* A Report of the National Bureau of Economic Research, Inc., Princeton University Press, Princeton, N.J., 1962, pp. 107-155; and G. J. Stigler, "Information in the Labor Market," *Journal of Political Economy,* 70 (October 1962, Supplement), pp. 94-96.

Manpower planning must take account of the variations in the effectiveness of market indicators and forces as between firms, occupations, and industries. It must know where and how market factors need to be supported and supplemented, and how the market can be made more effective through various public and private programs. The need for knowledge about the strengths and weaknesses of the market for manpower purposes shows why mobility studies and labor-market research can provide an important analytical underpinning for manpower planning and policy.

CHAPTER 3

∎∎

A New Concept of the Employment Service

∎∎

TRADITIONALLY, the Federal-State Employment Service has been viewed as a job exchange whose primary function is to find work for the jobless. That image of the Employment Service developed in the 1930's when, under the Social Security Act, the public employment exchange system was combined with the unemployment compensation program, and they were put under a common administrative unit, with the same local offices, staff, and source of financing. Merger of the State Employment Services with the administration of jobless benefits caused them to be popularly known as "the unemployment offices" and their effectiveness to be measured by the number of placements of unemployed persons credited to the Service.

In 1961 the Kennedy Administration commenced, for the large metropolitan areas, a program to separate the staff and local offices of the Employment Service from those for unemployment-benefit operations. In most of the fifty-two largest metropolitan areas in the nation the specialization has been carried further. Separate local offices have been established for professional and executive personnel, for commercial and other white-collar work, and for industrial and factory employment. In over 100 metropolitan areas, special Youth Opportunity Centers have been set up within the framework of the Employment Service. Every local office is to have identifiable youth services supplied by a staff qualified to work with youth, especially those who are disadvantaged in seeking employment.[1]

From time to time, Congress has placed other manpower duties on the Federal-State Employment Service system. Under the Manpower Development and Training Act, the State agencies are responsible for determining the occupations for which training under the Act is needed, for developing the training projects, for testing and selecting the trainees, and for job referral and follow-up after their training is completed. Under a program commenced in 1964, boys not attending school who are called up by Selective Service and who are unable for various reasons to meet the "mental" standards for induction into the Armed Services are referred to their local Employment Service offices for further testing and counseling designed to help them return to school, enter a training program, or find employment.

Despite such added responsibilities, the Federal-State Employment Service system continues to function largely as a job exchange for the unemployed. A 1963 survey of the activities of the public employment offices in five metropolitan areas in New York

[1] For a study of the historical development of the Federal-State Employment Service and its current activities and problems, see William Haber and D. H. Kruger, *The Role of the United States Employment Service in a Changing Economy*, the W. E. Upjohn Institute for Employment Research, Kalamazoo, Mich., February 1964.

State revealed the following distribution of staff time by program: 81 per cent on job placement; 12 per cent on counseling of workers; 4 per cent on labor-market information, occupational analysis, and industry service; and 3 per cent on community development and related activities.[2] The study found that the percentage of staff time spent on diagnostic and productive information about manpower demands and supplies (ranging from 2 to 6 per cent in the five areas) had not increased substantially during the previous fifteen years.[3] In 1957, a member of the Washington headquarters' staff estimated the time spent on Employment Service work for the country as a whole as follows: 75 per cent on placement work (taking job applications and job orders, selection and referral of workers for jobs, and verification of placements), 6 per cent on counseling, 5 per cent on labor-market information, 4 per cent on testing, and 10 per cent on all other services.[4]

Such an allocation of staff time seems inconsistent

[2] *A Study of the Programs of the New York State Employment Service*, McKinsey and Company, Inc., New York, April 1963, Chapter 3, p. 5. These figures do not include the time spent by the district staff preparing analyses of labor-market data collected by the local offices or that spent by the State Bureau of Research and Statistics in processing the material further for state-wide reports and submission to Washington.

[3] *Ibid.*, Chapter 4, p. 12.

[4] R. L. Thomas, "Major Aspects of the Public Employment Service," an unpublished report prepared by the present Assistant Director for Employment Service Administration, 1957, p. 1.

with a proper conception of an employment service as part of a broad manpower program. It is the thesis of this chapter that the Federal-State Employment Service needs a clear-cut definition of its mission that will highlight its manpower planning responsibilities. In recent years, with expansion in the range of its activities and in its counseling staff, the Service has been moving, in a piecemeal manner and without great unity of purpose, toward a new role and a new conception of its duties. Proper emphasis on manpower planning would make the activities of the Service more meaningful by providing them with new intellectual vigor and coherence. A planning mission for the Service's operations would result in greater stress on such long-range matters as occupational information and career guidance and less on simple job-placement activities than the New York State and the national figures seem to disclose. It would give the Service a longer perspective and a different set of priorities.

The way that a planning conception of the Federal-State Service would affect its program is discussed in this chapter. The next chapter deals with administrative, organizational, and personnel aspects of the new concept. The implications that a planning approach has for the thrust and content of the Employment Service will be examined under the following headings: information and communication; testing and counseling; job exchange and interarea clearance; and the Employment Service as the main instrument of manpower planning. The Federal-State Employment Service must be the basic instrument for carrying out the planning ideal set forth in Chapter 1.

Information and Communication

Properly conceived, the operations of a public Employment Service consist principally in supplying information to youngsters in school, adults, employers, the community, and governments. Information is gathered by the Service from surveys, studies, employer reports, day-to-day operations of the 1,900-odd local offices, and other sources. Its usefulness depends largely on the quality of the analysis and research on which it is based and the effectiveness with which it is packaged for and distributed to particular users and with which it is applied by them.

The Federal-State Employment Service is well situated to supply data of vital importance to individuals, firms, and the economy. Indeed, it is in a unique position to gather, process, and distribute much labor-market information. No other agency, public or private, has the necessary coverage, field staff, and facilities to ensure economy in collection, consistency of data, and expert analysis.

The significance of the informational activities of the Employment Service is evident from the range of material at its command. Among the kinds of data that the Service can supply are: facts and forecasts concerning employment opportunities in various occupations as a basis for career planning and training programs; the educational and other qualifications for different careers; inventories of workers who possess particular skills in an area; the actual and prospective effects of technological change on occupations and training; predictions of the size and composition of the nation's labor force; information on unemployment broken down by various classifications; data on job vacancies; classification of labor-market areas by degree of labor stringency or surplus; identification of current and prospective manpower shortages; research findings regarding the effectiveness of different aspects of the Employment Service's own operations; analysis of the costs and benefits of particular manpower programs; the requirements of the government and of government-financed programs for scientists and engineers; the present and expected structure of wage-benefit levels in different industries and occupations; factors that influence labor mobility and affect workers' willingness to transfer to other areas; and studies of labor turnover and factors affecting such turnover.

Good labor-market information should help to stimulate intelligent action by individuals and firms and by public bodies. To be fully effective, however, such information must be timely, continuously available, and directed at particular needs; and the potential users must have confidence in its reliability. Although career planning by individuals and manpower planning by firms may be a never-ending process, manpower information is most useful and effective if it is available in the right form at the right time.[5] And usually the potential users must be instructed in the ways that the information can be applied to achieve the greatest benefit from it. For that reason, careers pamphlets, vocational textbooks, a *Dictionary of Occupational Titles*, monthly issues of *Occupational Outlook*, masses of statistics, and other published material may fail to accomplish the stated purposes. For practical effectiveness, the data may require discussion, expert assessment, and assistance in application by school teachers, guidance counselors, employment interviewers, labor-market analysts, social psychologists, and others trained in the manpower field.

In the United States and abroad the use of advertising by the public Employment Service has been critically discussed. Expenditures by the State agencies for advertising have been less than 0.4 per cent of the total expenditures for Employment Service activities.[6] The corresponding figure has been 2 or

[5] As a staff report of the Select Subcommittee on Labor of the House of Representatives points out, "Pamphlets and other publications giving detailed, but readable, portrayals of skills required, training facilities, and trend of demand for a wide variety of occupations should be available for examination by individual workers visiting their 'community manpower centers.'" See *The Role and Mission of the Federal-State Employment Service in the American Economy*, Committee on Education and Labor, House of Representatives, 88th Congress, 2nd Session, U.S. Government Printing Office, Washington, D.C., 1965, p. 29.

[6] In 1963 the State services spent a total of $616,000 for advertising, of which $475,000 was for classified advertisements in newspapers. Some States have a flat prohibition on

3 per cent in recent years in Sweden, where expenditures for advertising in newspapers and on radio and television reached a peak of one million kronor[7] in the early 1960's.

The Swedish Labor Market Administration makes even more extensive use of other means of distribution. These include: a national vacancy list reporting new openings, published daily; a national vacancy list exclusively for teachers; a 40-to-60 page brochure (*Platsjournalen*), published every week, stating details about the jobs that are available; brief individual career leaflets; handbooks on training for jobs; and other career materials. The German Service issues weekly or twice a month, both nationally and for each State, employment gazettes (*Stellenanzeiger* and *Bewerberanzeiger*) setting forth job openings and workers available. In addition, a national gazette is issued twice a month for openings and applicants in the hotel industry, and special gazettes are issued, for example, covering graduating students from universities and technical schools.

Clearly advertising in newspapers or on the air has serious limitations for the presentation of detailed information and advice for career purposes or for appli-

---

advertising. (See *Public Employment Service*, Hearings before the Select Subcommittee on Labor, Committee on Education and Labor, House of Representatives, 88th Congress, 2nd Session, Washington, D.C., 1964, pp. 207 and 564.) Total Federal-State expenditures for Employment Service activities in fiscal year 1963-64 were about $172,000,000.

[7] Nearly $200,000.

cation in company manpower programs. Presumably the primary purpose of advertising in the case of the Federal-State Employment Service would be to encourage readers or listeners to visit the local office for more detailed information and advice. An incidental advantage in some States might be to provide a financial counterweight to extensive newspaper advertising by private employment agencies, which may cause newspapers to refer in their columns to the State Employment Service as the State "employment security agency" or the "unemployment bureau."

The Federal-State Employment Service has not supplied the general public with the kind of information needed for intelligent planning. The Federal Government should provide much more leadership and vision in this matter; central direction of data collection and analysis is essential for reasons of uniformity, expertise, and economy. Figures for an advanced State Service such as that of New York show the reorientation that is required for the development of a comprehensive, well-focused program. Of the 101 reports prepared by the New York Employment Service in a year, only eight were found in 1963 to be for employer or wider public use, and only one of the eight was for general circulation. This last is a monthly publication of labor-market information that a study, based on employer interviews, found to be inadequate as a basis for manpower planning.[8]

[8] *A Study of the Programs of the New York State Employment Service* (see n. 2), Chapter 3, p. 19.

A good information service is essential for directing vocational education and training programs, for sound employment counseling, for employer manpower planning, and for worker career selection. To improve Employment Service referrals and placement activities, it is necessary to have adequate information concerning current and prospective shortages and surpluses of manpower; changing occupational patterns and requirements; and rates of pay, benefits, and prospects for advancement in particular lines. As Leonard P. Adams remarks, a great and growing need exists for the sorts of information only a public employment service can supply, and the agency "has a greater opportunity to become the recognized community manpower center with respect to its information function than it has with respect to any of its other services."[9]

Testing and Counseling

Information about labor-market developments and occupations is of little benefit unless it is used to help solve the problems of people, firms, communities, and the nation. Both aptitude testing and vocational counseling are parts of a practical information program serving a long-range purpose. Testing attempts, by objective measurement of personal qualities, to aid in assessing a person's fitness for particular occupations or jobs.

[9] "The Public Employment Service," in J. M. Becker (ed.), *In Aid of the Unemployed*, Johns Hopkins Press, Baltimore, Maryland, 1965, p. 225.

Counseling has a dual purpose. One aim is the full development and satisfaction of the individual in his work. The other is promotion of the most effective use of the nation's manpower resources. The counselor serves those two aims by taking available information about occupational developments and about the particular individual (including test results) and suggesting the most appropriate kinds of career for him and the best way for him to prepare for a selected occupation or category of occupations. Good counseling can reduce ignorance and stimulate aspirations by opening up new occupational possibilities for persons. The individual must, of course, make his own career decisions and job choices, but a counselor can help to guide him intelligently. To perform such an educational service, a vocational counselor must be able to develop confidence in his expertness at individual assessments and in his knowledge of labor-market developments. In addition, he must be able to communicate with all sorts of persons. That is necessary if he is to guide and motivate them.[10]

The Employment Service in the United States has developed and applied aptitude and performance testing to a greater extent than has occurred in any other country. The Service's General Aptitude Test Battery (GATB), which requires about two and a

[10] The functions and contributions of employment counselors are described in *The Role and Mission of the Federal-State Employment Service in the American Economy* (see n. 5), pp. 11-14.

quarter hours to take, was administered to 762,000 persons in public employment offices during fiscal year 1963-64, and in addition it was administered to a large number of seniors in the high schools.[11] Still only half of the 21,200 high schools in the nation participate in the testing program offered by the State Employment Services. Performance tests, e.g., for speed and accuracy in typing and shorthand, and other tests besides the GATB were given in local offices to 1.5 million persons in 1963-64. The local employment offices in major cities have a special room in which to give tests. The U.S. Employment Service conducts research on its tests, and has developed a special nonverbal form of the GATB for persons with language handicaps.[12] Such a central unit is highly desirable for test development and research.

Tests can serve as an important aid to local offices in identifying and measuring talents and in selecting persons for referral to job vacancies. They help to ensure that the man and the job are well matched, that the persons referred to job openings meet the employer's standards of ability and performance, or,

[11] In the academic year 1961-62, the percentage of high schools participating ranged from 19 per cent in Texas to 96 per cent in New Hampshire. See *Public Employment Service* (see n. 6), pp. 82 and 543.

[12] A discussion of the GATB and some criticism of its application to some disadvantaged groups is contained in *Aspects of the Demonstration Program of Community Progress, Inc. in New Haven, Conn.*, Division of Special Programs, Office of Manpower, Automation, and Training, U.S. Department of Labor, June 29, 1964, pp. 9-11.

if they don't, that the employer knows what the deficiencies are and how they could be remedied. That, of course, is also an aim of vocational counseling.

Labor-market studies reveal the potential savings to workers, employers, and the national economy from testing and good counseling. Apparently a large proportion of the youths who enter manual employment take jobs without any career planning or even without much thought about the long-run prospects in that type of work.[13] As a consequence, dissatisfaction with the work is a major factor in the high turnover among young workers in industry.

In his 1965 *Manpower Report*, President Johnson stated: "Of every 10 high school dropouts, 8 reported that they had never been counseled by a school official or by a public employment office about job training or the kind of work to look for. Even among high school graduates, less than half reported that they had received occupational guidance."[14] That insufficient guidance is given to young persons is indicated by a survey in February 1963 showing that only 14 per cent of all youths got their first full-time job through school or a public or private employment agency. For nonwhites the figures was only 9 per cent.[15]

[13] See, for example, L. G. Reynolds, *The Structure of Labor Markets*, Harper and Brothers, New York, 1951, pp. 127-133.

[14] *Manpower Report of the President . . . 1965*, U.S. Government Printing Office, Washington, D.C., p. XI.

[15] Vera C. Parrella and F. A. Bogan, *Out of School Youth, February 1963*, Special Labor Force Report No. 46, Bureau of Labor Statistics, U.S. Department of Labor, Washington, D.C., 1965, Table B-5, p. A-10.

A number of European countries are far ahead of the United States with respect to systematic study of occupations and career guidance in the public schools. In Sweden, for example, vocational orientation is an integral part of the curriculum during the last three years of the basic school (student ages of 13, 14, and 15). In each of those three years, weekly periods are reserved for teaching about occupations, the world of work, and the necessary preparation for various careers. In the middle year, each student spends three weeks during term time working usually in two different jobs, mostly in private industry. The Employment Service arranges for such non-paid employment. In school, the students are prepared for the prevocational, on-the-job orientation by lessons. Afterward the pupils have follow-up discussions in class concerning their reactions, and they have individual consultations with the teacher relating this practical experience to their interests and abilities. The purpose of the program is work orientation; vocational choice presumably occurs at a later date. Specially trained vocational guidance teachers generally participate in the occupational and industrial instruction in those three school years.[16] In Norway the school curriculum contains even more weeks of industrial orientation and occupational discussion;

[16] Roughly the following amounts of class time are devoted to occupational material: 30 hours in the seventh grade, 20 hours in the eighth grade, and 10 to 15 hours in the ninth grade.

the student there writes papers on a number of occupations in which he is interested.

In Sweden and Germany, Employment Service counselors play a significant role in advising students about apprenticeships for different skilled trades and in placing students in jobs during their summer vacations. Thus, the Employment Services in those countries have contact with children in the equivalent of high school over a period of two years or more. In Sweden, through cooperation with college authorities, student organizations, and employer groups, most temporary placement of college students seeking trainee or vacation employment is handled by the Employment Service.

Great Britain made the mistake of turning over to Youth Employment Officers, attached to the county school boards and completely separate from the Employment Service, the vocational counseling and placement of boys and girls through age 18.[17] Consequently, the British Employment Service lacks the advantage of being able to offer employers a cross-section of new entrants into the labor force who have become acquainted with the Service's resources in advance, who have been counseled in groups and individually over a considerable period of time, and whose educational records are readily available to the Service.

[17] Actually, about 75 per cent of the schools in the United Kingdom are under this system. In the other 25 per cent the Ministry of Labour personnel do the school counseling.

Career guidance in high schools needs to be closely integrated with the regular vocational counseling of the Employment Service. As the Swedish authorities insist, career planning is a rather continuous process, often extending over a long period of time and is not, and should not be, just a discrete action taken at a point of time in a person's life. Preparatory information about occupations should be made available during the formative school years as part of the school curriculum, and career counseling for many youngsters may be needed long after they leave school. Follow-up advice may be especially important after experience on the first job.

Both the school authorities and the Employment Service have a strong interest in a smooth transition for youth from school to work. Because educational preparation and career guidance are interrelated, career advice in school and vocational counseling by the Employment Service after completion of school need to be closely integrated. Both should be based on the same information and both should have the same time horizon. Therefore, the Employment Service needs to be brought into closer relation to education and training of the young, and the school authorities need to be more aware of and concerned with the relationships between education and occupational requirements and advancement in employment. Both the Employment Service and the school authorities need to coordinate their thinking and policies with those of employers as the latter plan for their future manpower needs. Indeed, by providing a measure of leadership in manpower planning, the Employment Service can serve as a sort of consultant to employers in projecting their manpower requirements and developing programs to meet them.

The new concept of planning to achieve the most effective use of manpower and to provide an effective link between school and employment might make the term "manpower service" more appropriate than "employment service." It puts more emphasis on testing, counseling, and referral for further training and on the importance of long-term planning for the individual, the community, and the economy.

In the United States, school career guidance and the Employment Service are not well integrated. The State Employment Services do have "cooperative programs" with half of the 21,200 high schools in the country. Under those programs, a representative of the Service may give a talk to the seniors, who may also take the GATB. Of the 1.6 million seniors in 1964 in the 10,500 cooperating high schools, some 40 per cent (over 600,000) registered with the Service, about 22 per cent (350,000) were given some counseling service, and 6 per cent (over 100,000) were placed in jobs by the Service.[18] Senior year is, of course, too late to begin vocational guidance, and the attitude of the school staff toward the Service representative's "intrusion" varies from school to school.

In contrast, Germany has an extensive program of

[18] See W. E. Amos, "New Dimensions for Youth Services," *Employment Service Review*, 2 (May 1965), p. 2.

vocational guidance by the Employment Service in the schools during the last two school years. It includes providing students, teachers, and parents with comprehensive occupational information. Careers pamphlets are sent to about 600,000 students, and explanatory letters are sent to their parents. In 1963, problems of occupational choice were discussed in more than 32,000 school talks and in 5,200 special parents' meetings in which 60 to 70 per cent of the parents of school-leavers participated. On a voluntary basis, 84 per cent of all school-leavers consulted the Service's vocational guidance staff, which usually had two individual interviews with them, the second frequently including a discussion of test results. Some 65 per cent of all apprentice contracts in industry are concluded through the medium or with the assistance of the Service's vocational counseling staff of 1,500. In addition, 175,000 adults are counseled each year. The Service has some 120 university-trained psychologists, four-fifths of them in the Vocational Guidance Section.[19]

German employers work closely with the Service in its vocational guidance program, which they consider an objective and professional operation. The vocational guidance staff spends a considerable proportion of its time out of the office, visiting firms.

[19] The figures in this paragraph are taken from Bundesanstalt für Arbeitsvermittlung und Arbeitslosenversicherung, *Geschäftsbericht für das Rechnungsjahr 1963*, Nuremberg, Germany, pp. 27-31, and from interviews the author had with the staff of the Bundesanstalt.

Indeed, vocational guidance is the part of the German Service's program most highly praised by both employers and the general public. The employers appreciate the need for impartial, nationally oriented advice for the young, especially in communities where the range of employment opportunities is limited. It is probably true that the general labor shortage in Germany has caused more stress on vocational counseling and apprenticeship placement than would be the case were there significant unemployment in the economy.

An apparent weakness in the German program of vocational guidance for youth is the restricted role played by the school in career guidance and choice. The school may perform counseling with respect to further education, provide the student with general orientation to the world of work, and supply information about the student to the Service. Under the law, however, the Service (the Federal Institute for Labor Placement and Unemployment Insurance) is the only agency which may engage in vocational guidance and placement of apprentices.[20]

School participation in the vocational guidance program has the advantage that it can provide youth

[20] For material on vocational guidance in Germany available in English the reader is referred to: *Vocational Guidance and Occupational Training in the Federal Republic of Germany*, Issued by the Commissioner General of the Federal Republic of Germany at the International Labour Exhibition, Turin, 1961; and *Bundesanstalt für Arbeitsvermittlung und Arbeitslosenversicherung, Bundesrepublic Deutschland*, in German, English, French, and Italian, Nuremberg, 1961.

[63]

at an early stage with a second source of informed advice. In the United States, such participation would have the additional advantage that it would make use of a large supply of manpower trained for counseling. In early 1964, the number of full-time and part-time counselors on the staffs of the schools, the Employment Service, and rehabilitation and other public agencies was somewhat less than 50,000.[21] In that total, the full-time equivalent of counselors in the country's public secondary schools was about 27,000. In contrast, the total public Employment Service staffs performing some counseling duties were but some 3,000, of whom only about 1,700 were spending at least half of their work time in counseling activities, and about 1,000 of these were assigned full time to counseling. In 1964 about 1,000 more counselors were added to the staffs of the State Employment Services under a "crash" training program sponsored by the Federal Bureau of Employment Security and financed from Manpower Development and Training Act funds; most of the 1,000 were to be assigned to the new Youth Opportunity Centers.

Sweden has developed arrangements for the sharing of vocational guidance in the schools by the Employment Service and the school authorities. By law the County Labor Market Board and the County School Board have joint responsibility for the planning

[21] The figures in this paragraph are taken from *The Role and Mission of the Federal-State Employment Service in the American Economy* (see n. 5), pp. 16-19.

[64]

and supervision of vocational counseling in the basic or comprehensive schools in the county. At the national level, the Vocational Guidance Division of the National Labor Market Board works closely with the National Swedish Board of Education to develop informational material for school use and to plan and supervise vocational guidance by specially trained school teachers.

In order to have the Employment Service share vocational guidance in the schools, 600 teacher-counselors or career teachers are paid in part by the Employment Service, which is the main arm of the National Labor Market Board. This number compares with a total of 150 vocational guidance officers in the Employment Service offices themselves. The career teachers are graduates of teachers colleges, who have taken an additional five-month course arranged jointly by the National Labor Market Board and the National Board of Education. The Labor Market Board participates in the planning of the courses and provides some of the lectures. The training is given at the teachers colleges, and while they are taking the training the career-teachers-to-be are on reduced salary. The career teachers in each county have a one-day meeting each month to discuss such matters as information materials, new plans, or labour-market conditions.

The career teachers in Sweden receive both their normal pay as teachers and an extra salary from the Employment Service according to the number of individual students they counsel.[22] As their counseling expands, their normal teaching hours are correspondingly reduced. As a consequence, it is possible for career teachers to earn as much as the heads of the schools in which they teach.[23] Although this relatively high compensation may have seemed necessary at first to stimulate teachers to make the sacrifices necessary to become career counselors, the size of the combined salaries of some of them has been so large that the matter of proper compensation by the Employment Service is being examined.

The Swedish system of career teachers under the joint training, supervision, and compensation of the school authorities and the Employment Service provides a possible framework for cooperative development of occupational orientation and career guidance in high schools in this country. Obviously, certain modifications of the Swedish program would be necessary to fit American institutions and conditions. Considerable variation among the fifty States in courses, course content, salaries, and so forth, would be expected. Indeed, experimentation ought to be

[22] The 588 career-teachers reported that in the academic year 1963-64 they gave individual guidance to the following numbers of students: 23,239 in the 7th year of comprehensive schools, 42,961 in the 8th year, 36,340 in the 9th year, and 10,806 ex-students who were assisted in the immediate future following the end of their period in the comprehensive school.

[23] In Sweden it is not unusual for public employees to receive various kinds of "second" salaries or extra compensation from public and private sources.

invited. But basically such a cooperative program extending over, say, three high school years would be most valuable in bridging school and the world of work. Swedish experience demonstrates that. The sharing of special teacher training, salary costs, preparation of teaching materials, and other counseling requirements could be worked out in each State by the State school authorities and the State Employment Service. Presumably the Federal Government would meet the Employment Service's share of salary costs through the State Services, which are financed 100 per cent from Federal funds, and the U.S. Employment Service would supply centrally much of the manpower information, occupational leaflets, and similar material to both teachers and students.

It should be pointed out that the career-teacher program does not eliminate vocational counseling of youth in the employment offices. In Sweden in 1963-64 over 42,000 school pupils came to the local employment offices for interviews with vocational guidance officers; 4,600 of them were applicants for a job and many others were students in the noncompulsory (advanced) schools, which are not covered by the joint system of career teachers. In principle, the Swedish authorities consider it desirable to have young clients receive the same guidance and placement services as adult clients. Guidance arrangements are not separated by age in Sweden, and separate Youth Employment Agencies for placement purposes have been closed except in the three largest cities.

Vocational guidance may be especially needed for physically or mentally handicapped persons. But again, it may not be desirable to have separate offices or staffs for that purpose. In Sweden, efforts are made to mix disadvantaged workers with others in guidance, training, and placement activities so as to avoid unnecessary separation.

Job Exchange and Interarea Clearance

Consideration of the job exchange function brings out clearly the difference that the new concept of the Employment Service should make in its policies and operations. The exchange function—mistakenly called "placement"—consists in trying to match job openings and job applicants by selecting applicants and referring them to employers who have notified the employment office of vacancies. As explained early in this chapter, 75 to 80 per cent of the time of the Employment Service staff has been devoted to the "placement" function.

A properly functioning public employment exchange serves the following purposes:

1. Reduces the waste of time and money by workers in searching for jobs and by employers in recruiting workers.
2. Reduces imbalances between labor demand and supply, geographically and occupationally, by promoting labor mobility.
3. Increases employment by shortening the lapsed time in filling job vacancies.

4. Opens up a broader range of opportunities for workers and a broader range of supply for employers and, especially, improves the access of disadvantaged workers to jobs.

5. Improves labor allocation by helping to match requirements and abilities and carrying out the recommendations of counselors in referring applicants to jobs.

6. Provides valuable information for the Service and for manpower planning, with respect to such matters as occupational requirements, hiring standards, shortage and surplus skills, and rates of pay, all of which is helpful in vocational guidance. The information gathered by placement interviewers may also serve as an impressionistic check on the use of test results, the benefits of counseling, and the validity of selection methods used by the Service in referrals.

This list of purposes indicates that the exchange function needs to be guided by a concept of optimum labor mobility. Good counseling and good matching of applicants and vacancies should serve to reduce needless labor turnover and, thus, worker dissatisfaction and loss of employers' investment in employees. On the other hand, the Employment Service should promote job changing (labor turnover) when the results are a better fit of workers and jobs. Local employment offices also have to decide when it is desirable to fill vacancies (a) by moving workers into the locality under interarea clearance, (b) by attempting to draw former workers back into the labor force, (c) by shifting local jobless workers occupationally if their skills are partially transferable, and (d) by arranging some appropriate training of local jobless either by the community or by the employer.

Such alternatives indicate some of the possible differences of interest among employers, workers, the community, and the national economy. They also show the need to have the exchange function guided by a body of theory for deciding what is desirable and what is undesirable labor mobility, and to have a set of operating rules to promote proper mobility.

Because the Employment Service has not developed a clear-cut concept of optimum labor mobility it has no effective answers to charges that it is too interested in short-run placement at the expense of the long-run interest of workers, or that it is not performing a proper function when it refers an employed person to a higher-level position with another employer, or that referral of labor to vacancies outside the area is economically undesirable.

Possible conflict between long-run and short-run viewpoints frequently appears in the counseling and the job-referral parts of Employment Service operations. The counselor looks at a youth in terms of his whole career, and not just the job opportunities in a particular locality, from which he may move in a year or two. The "placement" officer is prone to think in terms of filling local vacancies to the fullest extent possible. Many of the openings filed with the Employment Service are casual or seasonal jobs that lead nowhere because they are not on any ladder of promotion. Most farm placements are of that sort, and the same is true of much domestic or household service. Of the total placements made by the Federal-State Employment Service in any one year, only about 30 per cent are in nonfarm jobs with over three days duration; about 55 per cent are farm jobs, and 15 per cent are jobs which last only one, two, or three days or even only part of a day. It is a nice question how frequently persons should be encouraged to interrupt career plans and preparations to fill such brief jobs.

Some of the over-three-day openings are on ladders of promotion so that they can lead to advancement. Others may be blind alley jobs. Again it is a nice question when and whether it is desirable to seek to place with another employer a person who is currently on a ladder of promotion in a firm or is likely to get on such a ladder soon. Perhaps one should say that the individual himself ought to decide according to his own judgment of his best interests, but good counseling might influence his decision, and the Employment Service should operate according to the public interest.

Clearly the job-exchange function should be an integral part of manpower planning for the most effective utilization of the nation's manpower. It should be coordinated with counseling. It should contribute to the over-all program by such means as providing labor-market information and helping disadvantaged workers to locate employment.

In the past, the Employment Service has gauged

its success largely by the number of job placements that the offices could claim credit for. Its so-called "penetration rate" is measured by the share of the Service's placements in the total of new hires. Estimates have been made for fiscal year 1960 showing the following distribution of hiring transactions according to the channels that workers used to obtain the jobs:[24]

	PER CENT
Direct application to the employer	36
Recruitment by relatives, friends, other employees of the firm	23
State Employment Service	16
Newspaper advertising	11
Private fee-charging agencies	4
Other channels	10
	—
	100

Thus, the Service's over-all penetration rate was 16 per cent.

By occupational groupings the estimated penetration rate of the Service varied as follows:[25]

	PER CENT
Professional and managerial	10
Clerical and sales	14
Skilled workers	8
Semi-skilled workers	11
Unskilled workers	30
Service workers	13

[24] See "Employment Service Participation in the Labor Market," United States Employment Service, U.S. Department of Labor, November 23, 1962, p. 4 (mimeo.).

[25] *Ibid.*, p. 3. Government and private household workers are not included in the calculations.

It is evident that referrals by the State Employment Services, generally speaking, account for three times as many of the new hires among unskilled workers as they do among skilled workers or professional and managerial personnel. In the building and printing trades the unions are a significant channel for new hires. Thus, the penetration rate for construction was only 9 per cent, compared with a penetration rate of 21 per cent for manufacturing and 14 per cent for trade and for finance, insurance, and real estate. Figures for thirty major metropolitan areas for fiscal year 1962 showed penetration rates in manufacturing alone ranging from 15, 16, and 17 per cent (Rochester, Syracuse, Buffalo, and San Diego) to 43 per cent in Memphis and 47 per cent in Phoenix.[26]

By comparison, the over-all penetration rate for Sweden is estimated at about 33 per cent[27] and for Germany about 40 per cent.[28] The penetration rate

[26] *Ibid.*, p. 6.

[27] Bertil Olsson, "Employment Policy in Sweden," *International Labour Review*, 87 (May 1963), p. 14. See also Hans Johansson, "Sweden," International Management Seminar on the Relation of the Public Employment Services to Management in the Recruitment of Personnel, Madrid, March 23-26, 1965, Organization for Economic Cooperation and Development, Paris, France, pp. 4-5 (mimeo.).

[28] In Western Germany between three and four million vacancies are filled each year by the labor exchanges, and the new hires amount to around eight million. See Reinhard Blasig, "Federal Republic of Germany," International Management Seminar on the Relation of the Public Employment Services to Management in the Recruitment of Personnel, Madrid, March 23-26, 1965, Organization for Economic Cooperation and Development, Paris, France, p. 9 (mimeo.).

for the Employment Service in Britain appears to be about the same as in the United States.

It is claimed that the Employment Service in an area must have a substantial penetration rate—25 or 30 per cent—in order to function effectively as a job exchange. It is also claimed that a substantial penetration rate in all branches of industry is necessary locally in order that the local employment office can have a sufficient variety of job opportunities to offer disadvantaged groups of workers, and that a substantial penetration rate in each branch of industry is required nationally in order for the Employment Service to obtain necessary information for the full range of occupations. Information on each occupation, it is argued, is needed for manpower planning, and some kinds of information can be acquired only if the Employment Service has the advantage of practical participation in the market process.

Those contentions are, however, of somewhat doubtful validity. The disadvantaged workers—school dropouts, members of minority groups, older workers who lack valuable skills—normally do not qualify for higher-level jobs in, for instance, professional, managerial, and skilled occupations. Mostly, what such workers need is to be hired into jobs that are the bottom rung on a ladder of promotion. For that purpose the Employment Service needs good employer contacts and a thorough understanding of the requirements for various jobs in the lower section of the job hierarchy. Local offices need to cultivate the growing areas of the economy, especially service

[74]

lines; there are many jobs in schools, hospitals, recreation, automobile and household services, etc. that do not require great skill or long training.

The staffs of the German and Swedish Employment Services spend considerable time on employer contacts. It is a fairly common practice for placement interviewers in the local employment offices in Germany to devote the morning to worker applicants and the afternoon to visiting employers.[29] In Sweden the Employment Service personnel seem to have more contact with local employers than is generally the case in the United States. The 1963 survey of the New York Employment Service found that those in placement activity spent 72 per cent of their time on "direct placement" (largely in-office activity) and only 8 per cent of their time on "employer promotion" (largely out-of-office visits).[30] Also a complaint by New York employers was that interviewers shifted around so much or left the Service so frequently that employers were reluctant to spend the time necessary to give an assigned interviewer full understanding of their manpower situation because that interviewer was likely to be replaced soon, frequently without telling the employer about the change.[31] A similar employer complaint exists in Sweden,[32] but with much less justification because the staff turnover

[29] In the United States apparently it is a common practice to spend one afternoon a week on employer visits.

[30] *A Study of the Programs of the New York State Employment Service* (see n. 2), Chapter 3, p. 5.

[31] *Ibid.*, Chapter 2, p. 12.

[32] See Johansson, "Sweden" (see n. 27), pp. 8-9.

in the Swedish Employment Service is only a fraction of that in many of our State Employment Services.

Undoubtedly knowledge accumulated through day-to-day functioning of a job exchange is helpful in providing information for manpower planning, counseling, etc. Job orders do supply data on such matters as changing occupational requirements, employers' hiring standards, developing occupational shortages, and prevailing pay structures. However, such information could, in large measure, be secured by other means, including visits to employers for that purpose. It is not necessary to have a continuing stream of job orders for doctors, nurses, teachers, or even secretaries in order to obtain information about present and prospective shortages and the effectiveness of various measures to overcome them; research may serve that purpose better.

More valid perhaps are contentions that a sizeable and well-balanced flow of job orders is required to achieve the job-exchange purposes of reducing the waste of time and money in job search and recruitment, shortening periods of joblessness, and improving labor allocation. But, assuming that a person is well counseled, one may ask what difference it makes, so far as labor allocation is concerned, whether he gets a particular job through the Employment Service or on his own by direct application.

A serious shortcoming of the Federal-State Employment Service has been its failure to develop an effective interarea and interstate exchange service. Although American workers are quite mobile geographically, only about 2.5 per cent of all nonagricultural placements in this country have been handled by the Employment Service under interstate, interarea, and interoffice (within an area) clearance. In contrast, in Germany interstate placements alone have been 10.5 per cent of all Employment Service placements in regular (not temporary) employment.

The clearance of workers and jobs between States is rather ineffective because the State Services and local offices are primarily concerned with operations within their own jurisdictions and because the procedures for interstate clearance are so slow and cumbersome as to discourage their use. For professional workers there is a network of offices linked by direct communication to speed up the clearance procedure, and close cooperation may exist between neighboring offices like the Professional Placement Centers in New York City and Newark, New Jersey.[33] Also, large-city offices may to some extent disregard official jurisdictions and State boundaries. For example, the Manhattan Apparel Industries Center in New York City serves as a national exchange for plant managers, industrial engineers, and designers in the men's and women's clothing industries; its Executive and Technical Unit issues an occasional "Profiles Bulletin" of trained personnel available and arranges placements all over the country. For summer resort operators, summer camps, and seasonal farm labor, the Service

[33] In 1965 there were ten separately located offices in eight States serving only professional applicants.

Industries Office in New York City provides a regional service covering New York, Connecticut, and New Jersey; the New York City office permits placement credit to be claimed by the offices in the localities where the New York City recruits go to work, and it takes only the order-holding credit even though it performs the complete service from order-taking to selection and, in some cases, to actual hiring.

To remedy the inadequate functioning of interstate clearance, the staff of the House Select Subcommittee on Labor proposed in December 1964 that the primary responsibility for the interstate clearance function be taken from the fifty State agencies and assigned to the U.S. Employment Service.[34] The staff pointed out that the Federal-State Employment Service is the only interlinked national network for gathering and disseminating information on job vacancies and job-seekers and, thus, is in a unique position to release workers and employees from the handicaps of imbalances in local labor market areas. The inter-area clearinghouse function is a vital one because workers are not well equipped to seek jobs on their own in other areas, and employers are usually not well equipped to recruit in other areas.

Instead of attempting to operate an interstate employment service involving the clearance of all occupations between all States, it would seem more desirable and practical for the Federal Government

[34] *The Role and Mission of the Federal-State Employment Service in the American Economy* (see n. 5), pp. 3, 51-52, and 70-71.

to start by following the German example. In 1954 the Federal Institute for Labor Placement and Unemployment Insurance in Germany established a Central Employment Office in Frankfort on the Main. It was designed primarily as a national clearing center for top-level executive positions in business and for the placement of university graduates (those trained for a profession and also liberal arts graduates).[35] In addition, there are units in six State Employment Offices (covering one or two State areas each), which handle professional and high managerial personnel wishing employment only within the State Office's jurisdiction and also handle openings for somewhat lower level managerial positions.[36] Both the Central and State Offices are located separately from other Employment Service operations.

The Central Employment Office in Germany functions largely by means of correspondence, by visits by six staff members to universities and technical schools, by publishing listings of vacancies and anonymous résumés of applicants, and by some use of the mass media, especially for high executive positions. The State Employment Offices operate within their State areas in much the same way; three to seven staff members visit the universities and colleges in

[35] The Central Employment Office (*Zentralstelle für Arbeitsvermittlung*) also serves as liaison for foreign placement of Germans and as a central exchange for trained personnel in the hotel and restaurant trade.

[36] Such as managers of stores, executive secretaries for managers of large businesses, etc., who are less likely to be recruited nationally.

[79]

their areas. Three or four months before graduation, some 40 to 80 per cent of the students (varying with the State) fill out résumé forms, on which they indicate the geographical area or areas in which they are willing to accept employment. Those whose area of placement interest is within a State are handled by the State Office, those with a local placement interest are handled by the local office in that city, and those with a placement interest spreading across State lines are the only ones handled by the Central Office. Good coordination exists among the three levels; the professional and managerial placements of State and major city offices have tended to expand more than those of the Central Office in recent years, partly because the Central Office was in full operation at an earlier date. Apparently, a quarter to a third of all new hires in the professional and managerial fields are handled through the three levels of the German Employment Service.

A strong case can be made for a national clearing center in the United States to service high-level managerial personnel, professional-school graduates, and college and university graduates generally. The market for such people as engineers, scientists, economists, doctors, business executives, hotel managers, and college graduates generally has become largely national in scope. For the most part, they have standard training or professional qualifications; and speed in placing them is generally not a major consideration. The relative scarcity of such personnel means that their allocation and utilization have great national interest. Probably they constitute the most important elements in the labor force from the point of view of national manpower planning. The Employment Service already has a professional office network, for which some national center is needed and on which a central exchange could be built.[37]

Such a central employment office for interstate matching of demand and supply in the professional and managerial fields could later expand into other fields if experience indicated that to be desirable. Consideration might also be given to service for the interstate placement of college and university students for summer vacation employment.

The Employment Service as the Main Instrument for Manpower Planning

The Employment Service must be the main operating agency in any program of manpower planning and its implementation, both locally and nationally. It should be the key institution for the collection, analysis, dissemination, and application of manpower information. And it should provide the major leader-

[37] New York City has an effective Professional Placement Center, whose staff visits college campuses in the city and upstate. In 1964, that Center received 6,775 applications from prospective and recent college graduates, and it assisted in placing 834 of them. In the late 1950's, the Center prepared and the State Service published a 90-page brochure entitled, *From Campus to Career, A Guide for Generalists* (majors in liberal arts or general business administration). The Center also conducts a sizeable college placement operation in summer camps.

ship in programs for the development and efficient use of the nation's manpower resources.

Such a role for the Employment Service means a new concept of its mission and its operation. It means more emphasis on research, planning, counseling, and training and retraining. It means more stress on services to youth in school, to employers seeking to solve their manpower problems, and to the community in the development and use of its labor resources. It means drawing employers, labor representatives, and community leadership more actively into manpower planning and policy decisions in the Employment Service. It means a broader conception and a longer view of Employment Service operations and a recognition of the responsibilities the Employment Service must undertake as a coordinating and leadership-supplying agency. And, of course, it means better trained and qualified personnel in the Service and a new set of criteria for judging success in the operation of local employment offices and of different branches of the Service.

This chapter has outlined a new concept of the Employment Service. In addition, two concrete proposals were suggested: career counseling in the high schools somewhat along the lines of the Swedish program for their basic schools, and the creation of a central employment office for professional, university-trained, and high-level managerial personnel, patterned after the German system with modifications for American conditions, which would serve as a national clearing center.

But more important than particular measures is the deliberate adoption of the new concept and its effective permeation throughout the whole Service— worked into budget allocations, into performance standards, into staff training, into procedures, and into daily operations.

Perhaps it is desirable that Congress embody the new concept in a revision and up-dating of the Wagner-Peyser Act of 1933, which created the Service. The staff of the House Select Subcommittee on Labor expressed the opinion in December 1964 that the Service needed a new, more explicit "mandate," for such purposes as supplying a guide for appropriations and answering critics who would confine the Federal-State Employment Service to the narrow role of an "unemployment office" or just a job exchange for low-skilled labor. The House Subcommittee staff claims: "Unless the Congress gives a forceful, comprehensive, and explicit statement of the responsibilities and scope of activities that it is assigning to the employment service, there will continue to exist public misunderstanding about the proper place of the service in our economy, and widespread failure to appreciate the importance of the service as a manpower agency."[38]

Experience demonstrates that a public employment service needs sufficient leeway to adjust its operations to changes that occur in the economy and in the structure and functioning of various levels of

[38] *The Role and Mission of the Federal-State Employment Service in the American Economy* (see n. 5), p. 69.

government. The Service must make its way in competition with other channels and means of labor recruitment and job-seeking. For that purpose it needs not only proper scope of operations and conception of mission but also well-coordinated organization of manpower functions and the development of a well-qualified staff. Those are the subjects of the next chapter.

CHAPTER 4

••

Organization and Staff for an Effective Service

••

THE new concept of the Employment Service propounded in the preceding chapter raises questions about the organizational arrangements and the quality of staff needed for comprehensive planning and effective operations. The Employment Service could not and should not be expected to be involved in every step in a man's whole work career. Consequently, problems arise concerning the coordination of other programs, such as general education and vocational training, with Employment Service policies. Furthermore, a better trained and higher quality staff is essential if the Federal-State Employment Service is to perform its manpower functions properly. The measures that are proposed here for staff improvement are chiefly those that the Federal Government could adopt.

Organization and Coordination

If one were starting a new employment service for the United States, undoubtedly a different organizational structure would be adopted. States are not economic entities; the patterns of labor mobility do not divide along State lines. For example, the northern half of New Jersey, in terms of worker commuting patterns, belongs to the New York metropolitan area, and the southern half of New Jersey is really part of the Philadelphia metropolitan area. Many States are too small in population for efficient operation of separately run Employment Services. They are too small, for instance, to have an economical and effective staff training program or research program. And the requirement that all Employment Service personnel be State employees (except those in the Washington headquarters and the Federal regional offices) has a distinct disadvantage in terms of the recruitment and development of a well-qualified staff. Salary levels for State employees are generally low and are surprisingly different, even for neighboring States. For their own employees, the States have made State boundaries severe barriers to mobility and professional advancement, both by seniority and benefit arrangements and by hiring and promotion practices.

A number of European countries converted communal or State services into national employment services after World War II. All European countries except Denmark, Italy, and Switzerland now have nationwide employment services, with their staffs all employees of the national agency. That promotes unity and coordination in manpower policies and operations.

After more than three decades of separate existence, the State Employment Services in the United States are well entrenched. It is not likely that two or more of them will merge, nor is there much possibility that the State systems will soon be amalgamated into a single national system. Thus, national manpower planning in the United States must assume the existence of fifty manpower operating units, with separate staffs and under the influence of fifty Governors and State legislatures.

The States are administrative units for many activities that have a bearing on manpower planning and operations. That is true of general and vocational education, health services, welfare programs, unemployment compensation, labor laws and their administration, conservation and industrial development, and economic and labor statistics. Although interagency cooperation at the State level may at times be difficult to accomplish, there is a single State executive—the Governor. The State administrative unit has some advantages along with its serious drawbacks.

In the manpower field in the United States there has been a tendency to start new programs in order to provide special impetus and funds for an activity not performed adequately, if at all, by the regular, old-line agencies. That, of course, was true during World War II, and has recently been the case, for example, with the retraining program under the Manpower Development and Training Act and the poverty program under the Economic Opportunity Act. The creation of such new national programs causes problems of coordination both in Washington and at the State level. To get fifty separate State programs to "sing out of the same hymnbook" is a real task of coordination in any program. Adding new programs expands the complications. Usually such "emergency" or special programs are eventually merged into the regular programs after they have proved their worth and shaken the old-line agencies "out of their bureaucratic ruts."

At the Washington level, two instruments for achieving coordination in manpower activities are the annual *Manpower Report of the President* and the President's Committee on Manpower, which is supposed to assess the interrelation of Federal programs in the manpower field in terms of available resources and requirements. However, the Federal Government has too many programs and agencies dealing with aspects of manpower planning to expect these two instruments to have a high degree of success in coordinating the policies and activities of all of them.

Germany and Sweden have achieved a considerable measure of cooperative action for their national programs by the device of establishing a manpower agency in the Ministry of Labor and Social Affairs (Germany) or the Ministry of Interior Affairs (Sweden), with authority placed in a tripartite board. The agency is given control over a wide range of manpower activities, and the "governing board" is composed of representatives of employers, labor, and government, selected by the national government. The State or County units have a similar "governing board" under the national board. Although constitutional difficulties might be encountered if an attempt were made to establish the German type of organizational arrangement in the United States, it may be instructive to examine both the German and Swedish patterns.[1]

The Federal Institute for Labor Placement and Unemployment Insurance (in Germany) is a self-administered corporation, governed at the top by two tripartite bodies with equal employer, labor, and Federal Government membership. One is a 39-man Administrative Council, which is a sort of legislative body dealing with general policies and the proposed budget. The other, a separate body, is a 9-man Executive Board, which is directly concerned with management matters, including formulating the budget, promoting personnel, and selecting the sites and designs of buildings for the Employment Service. The rulings of the Council and directives of the Board must be approved by the Minister of Labor and Social Affairs. There are also tripartite committees at the State and city levels to provide liaison between employers, workers, and local authorities at those points.

The Institute has by law sole authority to operate labor exchanges and to provide vocational guidance. In addition it performs the following related functions: recruits and places foreign workers, helps place physically handicapped workers, operates programs

[1] Similar organizational arrangements also exist in Belgium and Norway. It is noteworthy that at an international conference of management delegates from fifteen countries in March 1965 in Spain, management delegates from countries with a high degree of management influence in policy formation and in the administration of the country's employment service endorsed those particular arrangements. See *The OECD Observer*, August 1965, p. 31.

for adult training and retraining, provides subsidies for workers' housing, and administers unemployment insurance and children's allowances.

Thus in Germany the views of employers and organized labor find direct expression and voting influence at the very top. Employer and labor representatives on the Administrative Council and the Executive Board are nominees of their respective organizations for 4-year terms; they are part of the top management and are not just advisors. They act on the budget, appointments, training programs, buildings, research proposals, and so forth. The tripartite State and city councils find that their possibilities for influencing policy or budgets are much more limited. A local council can, of course, suggest a training program and is consulted on appointments in its area. The nine State councils and the city councils have, however, little significant direct influence on the budget or on nationally formulated policies.

In Sweden, employers and organized labor also have a direct influence on manpower programs, and the national manpower agency (the National Labor Market Board) has wide-ranging responsibilities, including measures for creating employment. The main outlines of manpower policy are legislated by the Parliament. Within those outlines the National Labor Market Board shapes policy and works out specific programs to put the policy into effect.

The National Board's responsibilities include: supervision of the Employment Service; management of vocational guidance and vocational rehabilitation;

all but the teaching aspects of retraining; operation of a program of financial incentives to encourage geographical mobility of workers; the issuance of starting permits for building; advice on the location of new factories; control of the voluntary unemployment insurance societies; and the handling of applications for deferment of military service. In addition, the Board has certain selective means to increase demand and employment. They include: the starting of emergency public works financed out of credits at the Board's disposal; the placing of orders for regular public works (such as roads), using special funds available to the Board; and the releasing by the Board of tax-exempt reserve funds of private firms for employment-creating investment.

The National Board is composed of ten members appointed by the King-in-Council. They are: two employees of the Board (the Director General, who is chairman, and the Deputy Director General); two representatives nominated by the employers' confederation, two by the federation of trade unions, one by the salaried workers' organization, one by the Swedish Confederation of Professional Associations, and two who traditionally represent agriculture and employed women. One or more of the ten is likely also to be a member of Parliament. The Board must approve the budget before it goes to the national government for action.

One reason for explaining the National Board's composition is to indicate its mixed character and the extent of employer and organized labor representation. The Board has been less prone to divide along employer and labor lines than has been true in Germany. The representatives feel free to follow their own convictions. Normally, the National Board meets twice a month, and, with only a few exceptions, the Board's decisions are unanimous. In fact, the Board and the Employment Service, which is its main instrument, enjoy strong support from both organized industry and organized labor.[2] Employers and organized labor are also represented on certain advisory delegations within the structure of the National Board.

The present Director General is a dynamic person, and his position carries significant political influence by virtue of the fact that the Board allocates roads and other public works. He has followed a policy of partial decentralization, with considerable delegation of functions to the twenty-five County Labor Market Boards. Their policies must, however, follow the lines laid down by the National Board.

The County Boards are appointed by the King-in-Council after nomination by the Director General of the National Labor Market Board. Each County La-

[2] Business management has at times been concerned that the Board may be attempting to cover a larger proportion of new lines, especially in the upper levels of management, than is necessary for an effective manpower policy. See, for example, Hans Johansson, "Sweden," International Management Seminar on the Relation of the Public Employment Services to Management in the Recruitment of Personnel, Madrid, March 23-26, 1965, Organization for Economic Cooperation and Development, Paris, France, pp. 7-11 (mimeo.).

bor Market Board consists of a chairman, usually the Governor of the County, and five other members, three of whom traditionally represent the organizations of employers and workers. The Governors are busy men, but apparently they do attend at least half of the Board meetings. A forceful County Director might not submit many questions to his Board, and the County Boards are circumscribed by national policies and national budget constraints. Within those limits, however, they can influence many practical decisions on such matters as worker retraining programs, employment for handicapped workers, and the volume and location of small emergency works (the large works, like roads, are allocated by the National Board). The County Boards receive constituents' views on needs for action within the County on such matters.

Certain features, especially of the Swedish set-up, would seem to have application in the United States. In this country, a tripartite Federal Advisory Council, established in the 1930's, supplies advice to the Bureau of Employment Security, and each State has a similar tripartite advisory council to make recommendations to the Governor and legislature. Unfortunately most of the time and attention of such advisory units has been devoted to unemployment compensation, on which labor and management often divide sharply. Thus, the Employment Service and manpower policy have tended to be either neglected or caught up in conflict over extraneous issues.

The Federal-State Employment Service needs

[93]

from employers and labor much more continuous understanding, consultation, and participation in policy formulation than is provided by the present fitful and feeble advisory arrangements. Administrative boards, with management, labor, farm, and other public representation, as in the Swedish set-up, should be established at the Federal and State levels. In that way the Employment Service would be able to draw more effectively on its customers for information, positive policy recommendations, cooperation in the implementation of policy, and support for high-quality service. And a high degree of participation in policy formation by non-salaried representatives of management and labor on an over-all administrative board at both Federal and State levels would provide additional links between those levels within the Service, would challenge bureaucratic complacency with fresh views, and would help to improve the coordination between public and private manpower planning.

To have representatives of client interests on an official government board participating in the management of a program is not a common pattern in the United States as it is in Sweden. However, there would seem to be no basic objection to that pattern in this particular case. The Employment Service is not a regulatory board. It provides services, focussing on the individual, that are closely connected with the operations of business management, labor unions, and community services, and which vitally affect the community and the whole economy. For that kind of a program, client representation on management boards seems quite appropriate and highly desirable.

Because there are fifty separate State Employment Services making up the Federal-State system, the administrative structure needs strong regional units for certain functions. Most States are too small to be fully effective with respect to such functions as staff training, research, preparation of informational material for vocational guidance, promotion of professional interests of trained staff, interchange of knowledge and experience, and manpower planning for a regional area.

Each of those functions is growing in importance. A regional unit might serve to promote them as a group. The next section contains a proposal for four regional staff training centers—one for the Northeast including the Middle Atlantic States, one for the South, one for the Midwest, and one for the Mountain States and the Pacific Coast. Chapter 8 presents suggestions for strengthening manpower research and research training at universities in a region. Some connections probably should exist between the training of State staffs, particularly for higher-level professional and managerial positions in the Service, and manpower research (and the training for such research) at the regional level. Such a connection would help to raise the level of professional interest and the attractiveness of the State Services.

Labor mobility, guidance information, and manpower planning are matters in which the States of a region have a common interest, and effective means of discussing and implementing policies on these matters at a regional level are now lacking. A well-staffed regional unit, responsive to State and regional needs, is clearly required.

Staff Development

Manpower planning and utilization programs require a competent, well-trained staff in the Employment Service. Placement interviewers must know the skill content of jobs and employers' specific requirements, be able to judge the capabilities of persons under particular conditions, and be competent to cope with people from a wide variety of backgrounds and positions, including top management. Vocational counselors must be able to identify aptitudes and think in terms of attributes common to certain jobs so as to indicate the full range of employment for which a person might qualify. They must be able to interpret test results, be familiar with the range of facilities for developing workers' skills, and be capable of relating personal interests and skills to successful occupational performance and to future trends in demand for specific skills. Managers of Employment Service offices need to be well grounded in all aspects of the Service, able to provide leadership in the community, and skilled in modern techniques of management for such a public operation. All interviewing and managerial personnel should be proficient in labor-market analysis and in the application of manpower data and research findings.

The staffs of most State Services fall far short of these desired standards of ability, training, and supervisory qualities. There is, of course, considerable variation among States. New York, Michigan, and California, for example, have some very capable persons in their Employment Services. Generally speaking, the State Services did attract many able and highly motivated employees in the 1930's. The recruits of the 1930's have worked up into top levels of the organization and are approaching retirement age. Persons recruited in the 1940's and 1950's who still remain employees of the Service are, generally speaking, somewhat lower in quality. During the 1960's some States have been recruiting able young persons, but have found great difficulty in retaining them for more than one or two years.

The State Services have been handicapped in recruiting and retaining properly qualified staff. The principal handicaps have been low salaries, limited opportunity for professional advancement, and inadequate staff training and development programs. Low quality of personnel and high turnover have given many State Services a bad "image."

By any standards the turnover of staff in many State Services is excessive and most wasteful. Indeed, turnover of personnel is reported to be a problem common to all States.[3] A vice president of

[3] "U.S. Reply to MS/M/201/138, Role of Employment

industrial relations for a steel company has stated that the turnover in the St. Louis Employment Office in 1963 was 21.7 per cent, whereas rates for a similar work force in industry would be in the neighborhood of 3 to 4 per cent.[4] In New York City offices, turnover rates have averaged as high as 30 to 40 per cent a year. In the Manhattan Apparel Industries Center, for example, out of a staff of 108 interviewers in mid-1965, there were 45 (or 42 per cent) who had been with the Employment Service less than two years. For many persons a job in the Employment Service is a first step to better-paying and more promotion-promising employment in private industry.

High staff turnover has many unfortunate effects. Not only does it make personnel and training costs excessively high, but it also tends to dilute staff training because of discontinuities and the need to handle large numbers. A high quit rate has a bad effect on staff morale and damages relations with worker clients and with employers. Confidence in the continuity and quality of service drops when employer-contact personnel repeatedly leave the Service.

Low pay scales and insufficient differentiation in

Services," Organization for Economic Cooperation and Development, Paris, February 1, 1965, p. 28 (mimeo.).

[4] Statement of John R. Huntley of Granite City Steel Company, in *Public Employment Service*, Hearings before the Select Subcommittee on Labor, Committee on Education and Labor, U.S. House of Representatives, 88th Congress, 2nd Session, U.S. Government Printing Office, Washington, D.C., 1964, p. 397. Missouri has been among the lowest States in pay scales for Employment Service personnel.

salaries according to skills and training have hurt the Employment Service in the recruitment and retention of able personnel. Salaries in the State Employment Services must conform to the scales for other State employees. For the basic job (employment interviewer), low-paying States have scales 20 per cent or more below those of high-paying States in the same region.[5]

Among the States that have low salaries for their regions are Pennsylvania, Delaware, Ohio, West Virginia, Kansas, and Missouri. (Missouri has long been the bottom State for salaries of employment interviewer and employment counselor.) The relatively low pay scales in Pennsylvania have made it especially difficult to recruit and hold high-quality personnel in large cities like Philadelphia and Pittsburgh. Philadelphia Employment Service personnel in the lower ranks have left for jobs in private industry at salaries as much as 20 or 30 per cent above their Employment Service pay. As a result, the State Employment Service is left with either the lower quality employees or those who have special reasons for resisting better pay and promotion possibilities in private industry.

Rigidity of State salary administration has also hampered recruitment of qualified vocational counselors for State Services. Some States, including New York and California, have not been permitted to pay

[5] See *State Salary Ranges*, published for January 1 and July 1 each year by the Division of State Merit Systems, Department of Health, Education, and Welfare, Washington, D.C.

fully trained counselors a higher starting salary than they pay entering employment interviewers, who generally have much less academic training.[6] Other States have totally inadequate salary differentials for well-qualified counselors and low ceilings on the highest counselor salaries. In addition, fully trained counselors have a relatively low professional status in most State Employment Services because of the wide mixture of their duties, poor office arrangements, and professionally frustrating workloads—as many as 12 or 13 interviews a day compared with a standard of no more than 6 a day abroad.[7] A consequence of these difficulties is that qualified counselors in the Employment Service tend to be drawn into school and other counseling where the pay is at least $1,000 a year higher, and the Employment Service has to use counselors who do not meet professional standards. Of the 1,700 persons on Employment Service staffs who were spending at least half time on counseling early in 1964, only about two-thirds even had college degrees.[8]

[6] A sampling of interviewing staff personnel in thirty-one States in 1963 showed that their total years of formal education averaged 14. Of the sample, 34 per cent had Bachelor degrees, 5 per cent had graduate degrees, 6 per cent were currently studying for a degree, and 65 per cent left college before getting a degree.

[7] For a discussion of these matters see *The Role and Mission of the Federal-State Employment Service in the American Economy*, Committee on Education and Labor, House of Representatives, 88th Congress, 2nd session, December 1964, U.S. Government Printing Office, Washington, D.C., 1965, pp. 11-25.

[8] *Ibid.*, p. 16.

Another serious defect in the personnel programs of State agencies is inadequate staff training and development. This has apparently been a significant factor contributing to the inability of States to maintain a well-qualified staff.

Generally speaking, the Employment Services in the United States spend much less time and effort on staff training than is the case in Germany, Great Britain, or Sweden. The same is true of professional and executive development. The difference that a well-conceived program of training and development can make is evident in the top staffs in those countries. Generally speaking, the directors of large city offices and heads of State offices in Germany, the regional controllers and deputy controllers in Great Britain, and the directors of County Labor Market Boards in Sweden are persons with an impressive breadth of knowledge, range of competence, and mastery of their jobs. The same is true of top personnel in the central headquarters.

A brief explanation of the German training program, which is the most advanced, illustrates some directions in which our Federal-State system should move. New recruits, whatever their age and ultimate position, undergo a three-year training period. Each office in a large city has a head of training; there are classrooms for training purposes in the building; and training classes for new employees are held during the week. New employees who are considered possibilities for promotion to high-level positions have two periods of three-months each at a full-time residence training center during their first three years of employment.

The German Service has two specially designed, resident training centers, one at Lauf, which is a twenty-minute drive from the national headquarters at Nuremberg, and the other at Münster-Mecklenbeck. A third training center is being planned. The center at Lauf, opened in 1957, is for the training of higher-level personnel, including those who are directors of city offices, chiefs of departments in large city offices, and heads of smaller local offices subordinate to a large city office. The Mecklenbeck center is for training middle management, the cut below those trained at Lauf. The Lauf center has dormitory, classroom, library, and eating facilities for sixty residents and, in addition, handles occasional small, nonresident groups. The training period at Lauf for employees who have completed their three-year training is usually two weeks, and they are generally trained in groups of thirty or less.

The German training program provides for new recruits a thorough indoctrination and grounding in various aspects of the Service. During their training period they serve under a senior person who assumes responsibility for their development. In vocational guidance, for example, the junior employee in training will prepare and deliver a lecture to a group of school children; the lecture will then be examined and criticized in detail by the supervising senior man. The carefully prepared and extensive training program convinces new recruits that they are part of a well-run institution in which a definite career or profession can be pursued on a long-term basis. For those with years of experience in the Service, resident training periods serve to bring them abreast of new techniques and research findings, help to give them a broader perspective, and permit an exchange of experience and views during the discussion periods following formal presentations by specialists. Through the records made at the training center, the abilities of participants come to the attention of the higher authorities. Training records are part of the personal data used in selecting persons for appointment to higher positions. The residential training program also permits personnel in the same position or stage of development, but from widely different geographical locations, to become well acquainted with each other and with problems elsewhere in the Service. Like large firms in this country, the German Service makes a conscious effort to have employees with good promotion possibilities circulate in order to gain varied experience and meet new challenges during periods of employment in different positions and functions of the Service in various parts of the country.

Two other features of the German program contribute to the training and development of staff. The system of a thorough, two-week "inspection" of each local office every two years by a specially appointed team of five serves a training function for both the team members and the office director. It is really a review and analysis culminating in a report with recommendations, which is discussed at various levels in the Service. The second feature is the stress that the German Employment Service program places on field visits by staff, especially interviews with executives in industry. Heads of offices are expected to be thoroughly familiar with the manpower problems of business firms and to be able to converse intelligently with high industrial executives about their manpower problems.

Employers in Germany and Sweden have suggested that, as part of every new employee's training, he spend some time in the employment offices of at least two firms, one of them a nonmanufacturing operation. Undoubtedly that would be a desirable addition to the German training program, and also to Employment Service training in this country.

The Federal-State Employment Service in this country badly needs four or five residential training centers similar to the one at Lauf in Germany. Presumably they should be located so that one would serve the States in each of four regions—the Northeast including the Middle Atlantic States, the South, the Midwest, and the Mountain States and the Pacific Coast. Presumably a regional training center, such as the one at Lauf, should be directed at training for the higher-level positions in the State Services.

The advantages of such residential training centers in this country would be much the same as those that have been achieved in Germany. They would help to breathe new life into the State Services and to attract and hold good new recruits who have long-run career and professional interests. By serving to reduce parochialism, they would increase the mobility within the Federal-State Service of able staff, both within a State and between States. Some of the managers of local employment offices have never visited offices outside the county, or discussed mutual problems with office managers outside the State, or had any contact with academic experts who have made studies that have a bearing on the operations of an employment office.

In recent years, the Federal Bureau of Employment Security has arranged, on an ad hoc basis, for a few universities to give one- and two-week seminar programs for Employment Service personnel, usually in the summer. Michigan, Cornell, and Princeton have once or twice offered such seminars for high-level staff drawn from the fifty State Services. However, such occasional seminars, with the sessions mainly led by faculty members from various universities, are no substitute for a system of permanent regional training centers. Such centers could, of course, be tied in with universities that serve as regional manpower research centers, but the case for them rests on the important training purposes they would serve.

A regional training program would help to lower artificial barriers to staff communication and mobility between States. Since the Federal Government finances the full salaries of State Service personnel, the House Subcommittee's staff has proposed that Congress take action to ensure freer movement of experienced personnel among the separate agencies and between the State agencies and the Federal Bureau of Employment Security. Regional training centers would be one positive and effective means toward that end. The Subcommittee's staff proposed legislation "that would prescribe a system permitting the transfer of personnel," both interstate and Federal-State, without loss of rank, seniority position, or accumulated pension and other benefits.[9] Transfer without loss of benefit rights is often an important consideration. Rank and length of service are matters of State civil service legislation or practice.

Effective Manpower Administration

The Federal-State Employment Service can be only as good as its staff. For services like labor-market information, vocational guidance, applicant referral, manpower advice to employers, and community manpower planning, staff is the decisive factor.

The drive to improve the personnel in the Federal-State Employment Service that began in 1961 can be expected to show significant results only over a considerable time span. State practices cannot all be altered over night. To elevate the level of a government agency's work force by recruitment, training, and new stimuli and programs is a long-term undertaking. Existing work forces tend to recruit, indoctrinate, discourage, and promote newcomers in line with their own image. Only gradually can one expect to change the public's conception of a government

[9] *The Role and Mission of the Federal-State Employment Service in the American Economy* (see n. 7), p. 53.

agency that has been in operation for more than three decades. A part of the German public still connects that Employment Service's pre-war buildings with their wartime use by the Nazis for the forced allocation of labor.

The problem of improving the staff and the public's conception of the Service needs to be attacked on many fronts. Two measures have been stressed in this chapter. The one, to provide client representation in top policy-making and management at the Federal and State levels, would bring in new viewpoints, new interests, and new channels of communication. The other, to provide new regional training arrangements for the higher-level positions in the Federal-State Service, would help to attract and hold personnel with high talent and improve their competence in Employment Service operations.

The Employment Service advises employers about ways to reduce labor turnover and to plan for future manpower requirements. Its precepts should be applied to its own problems. Then its recommendations to employers would carry more conviction.

Large business concerns have extensive programs of training and executive development. The Federal-State Employment Service should likewise adopt and apply the lessons of modern industrial relations and personnel management. The Service is competing with industry and other branches of the economy for competent staff. Without a well-qualified staff, efficient operations are not possible.

....

CHAPTER 5

Planning on the Demand Side

....

BASIC to manpower planning is an analysis of future needs for various types of trained personnel. The projected requirements of industry, government, households, and other employing units must be compared with estimates of future supplies qualified to meet those requirements.

Essentially, manpower planning is a matching problem. If, for an occupation requiring lengthy training, demand and supply as projected over a five- or ten-year period are significantly out of balance, action may be necessary to stimulate an increase in the qualified supply in order to meet the expanding demand at the proper time. If a projected declining demand for an occupation is likely to result in greatly excessive supply in future years, measures to help correct that imbalance need to be taken.

Also, adjustments in the composition of total demand may facilitate a matching by skill types. Employers may need to revise their skill-mix, for example, if a rapid expansion in the supply of workers with a certain combination of skills and talents would be difficult to achieve. At the other end of the skill range, special efforts may be necessary in order to obtain employment for unskilled workers who suffer from handicaps in the regular job market.

Of course, market forces greatly aid in the matching of manpower requirements and manpower supplies. Workers move to take advantage of expanding job opportunities and attractive pay. Greater opportunities in certain lines for which large numbers of women are qualified (like teaching, nursing, or stenographic services) may enlarge the supply by drawing women from the household into gainful employment. Scarcity of a particular type of labor, accompanied by a relative rise in its pay, causes employers to try to use cheaper substitute labor. Much of a projected imbalance of demand and supply may tend to be eliminated by flows of new entrants, by minor shifts in the existing labor force, and by changes in employers' operating methods, all of which occur without any planning or special effort by government agencies.

However, as already explained, the market may not be very effective in arranging the optimum allocation and utilization of the nation's labor force. Workers and employers are hampered by ignorance and uncertainties. In practice, market indicators may be misleading; present wage-benefit levels may furnish poor directional signals for the selection of a career to be pursued over the next three or four decades. Also, given all the barriers to mobility, the market unaided may be slow in adjusting supply to developing demand. That can be especially true for the professions, where the lead time from occupational choice to full preparation may be a decade or more, where occupational choices are subject to many nonmarket influences, where the annual inflow of qualified personnel normally is only 4 or 5 per cent of the total stock, and where training for the profession is heavily subsidized by government and private gifts.

Full employment in European countries has not eliminated the need for manpower planning by the central government and by the States and localities. Indeed, because the malallocation of resources is more evident under full employment, with manpower bottlenecks and inefficiencies clearly restraining economic growth and pushing up prices, the case for long-range manpower planning is likely to be clear and strong under general labor stringency.

In manpower planning, projections of occupational demand serve a number of important purposes. By indicating the outlook for employment in various occupations, they provide essential information for career counseling and vocational choice. Estimates of the needed number of workers with particular types of skill and knowledge are basic information for programs of general and vocational education. Educational planning should be guided, at least in part, by manpower requirements of the economy.

In addition to providing aid for career selection and educational policy, data on future occupational trends can help to guide decisions of private industry, the government, and community leaders. The manpower outlook by occupation and area is basic for company programs of manpower planning, employee training, and location of factory and office buildings. In its vast operations the Federal Government also needs to take account of projections of manpower requirements for the economy as a whole. That is true not only of decisions with respect to selection and training for the armed services but also with respect to civilian programs that place heavy demands on professions involving long training, such as medicine, science, and engineering. Competing for scarce manpower resources, a program like the space effort may expand rapidly only at some expense, say, to teaching in institutions that train future supplies of scientists and engineers. And data on rapidly growing or declining types of employment are of great importance not only for local policies concerning public education and vocational training but also for decisions with respect to community development and the diversification of local industry.

This chapter focusses on aspects of manpower planning on the demand side. The next chapter deals with the adaptation of supply to demand. Actually, manpower demand and supply are so interrelated that it is difficult to think of one apart from the other. In considerable measure it is projected changes in one relative to the other in specialized categories—the imbalances in demand and supply for distinct occupations or skill classes—that are important for planning purposes and for manpower programs.

Discussion of demand aspects in this chapter will center on four subject areas: (1) problems of forecasting requirements, (2) modifications in hiring standards, (3) job creation for special needs, and (4) manpower planning and employment creation. Supply considerations do enter into all those subjects, and are the primary reason for giving special attention to the last three.

Problems of Forecasting Requirements

Prediction of occupational requirements for ten years or more in advance is a hazardous undertaking. The future is uncertain, and the longer the period of projection, the greater is the range of possible variation. Occupational demand is affected by many factors, some of which, even after great effort, can be foreseen only imperfectly.

Nevertheless considerable progress has been made in the art of forecasting manpower needs by occupation and skill categories. Much has been learned from experience with systematic projections of long-term manpower requirements in this country and abroad since the United States Bureau of Labor Statistics began to study the matter in 1940. Even the first rough predictions for 108 occupations that the BLS made in 1948 were, in almost three-fourths of the cases, reasonably close to the actual developments recorded in the Census of 1960.[1] In only 9 out of 108 occupations did actual employment change move in the direction opposite to that forecast. By 1965, the *Occupational Outlook Handbook,* issued by the BLS

[1] See Harold Goldstein, "An Evaluation of Experience in Long-Term Projections of Employment by Occupation," *Proceedings of the 21st Interstate Conference on Labor Statistics, June 25-28, 1963, San Francisco, California,* U.S. Department of Labor, Washington, D.C. 1963, pp. 210-219.

every two years, was describing future employment opportunities in nearly 700 occupations, and the methods of forecasting manpower requirements had greatly improved since 1948.

The methods for predicting requirements by occupation and skill level can be grouped into three general categories: statistical, econometric, and judgmental. The statistical methods include extrapolation of past trends into the future; use of standard growth curves for an industry and the translation of industry figures into occupational needs according to current occupational mixes; and application of standard ratios of occupational personnel to projections of population in the relevant categories. For example, the requirements for elementary school teachers would be based on the expected number of children 5 to 12 years of age and an assumed pupil-teacher ratio, and the requirements for doctors would be determined by a patient-doctor ratio applied to the expected population, with possibly different doctor-patient ratios used for particular age groupings and population densities.

Econometric methods use comprehensive models of the economy. The nation's Gross National Product and its major components are projected into the future, providing estimates of the total demand for goods and services year by year. The estimates of total product demand are then translated into manpower requirements by industry and by occupation. Allowances can be made for the effects of various assumed rates of unemployment upon manpower demand in individual industries.

Although the BLS uses statistical and econometric methods in the process of making industry and occupational projections of labor demand, the final results are essentially judgments based on a composite assessment of the influence that a variety of factors have on levels of industrial and occupational employment. The material used in formulating the final judgments may include, in addition to trend and econometric data, information from employer surveys, results from studies of innovation in products and production techniques, analyses of the impact of automation and other technological changes, and background material from discussions with representatives of industry and unions.[2]

The BLS stresses that its long-term projections of employment by occupation are prepared for the guidance of individuals in the choice of a career. For that purpose, exact quantitative estimates are not necessary. A verbal statement of relative order of change is usually sufficient. However, actual numerical projections for each occupation and industry are carefully recorded in technical memoranda, along with the facts, reasoning, and calculations that go

[2] See R. A. Gordon (ed.), "Long-Term Manpower Projections," Proceedings of a Conference Conducted by the Research Program on Unemployment and the American Economy, University of California (Berkeley) in Washington, D.C., June 25-26, 1964, Institute of Industrial Relations, University of California, Berkeley, California, 1965, p. 24 (mimeo.).

into each projection.[3] Such material provides a basis for evaluating experience and for learning from mistakes. The quantitative estimates that are made may be desirable for the guidance of education and training authorities.

In the field of forecasting occupational requirements much remains unsettled. Current occupational classifications of the Census may be unsatisfactory for arriving at aggregates of all-industry needs by type of skill or knowledge. Aggregates in terms of levels of instruction would be desirable for purposes of developing specific training programs. Skill as such may be difficult to define and standardize, so that classification by skill levels may produce rather ill-defined aggregates. Lack of uniform standards of quality in manpower estimates makes it difficult to arrive at a figure for shortage or surplus in an occupation at a particular point of time. Often in service lines a projected shortage seems to disappear because less qualified substitutes are used, say, for teachers, engineers, or nurses.[4]

Beyond ten years, quantitative forecasting of occupational needs confronts serious obstacles. Within a decade there is considerable stability in the occupational pattern of many industries. Innovations that alter production techniques and occupational

[3] Goldstein, "Long-Term Manpower Projections" (see n. 2), p. 8.

[4] The *ex ante* gap is eliminated *ex post* by the acceptance of a substandard supply. It is rare to find that jobs remain vacant for any length of time because a fully qualified person is not available.

mixes within industries can be known for as long as five years ahead. Forecasting of such technical advances may be extended a few years by better systems of information and analysis. But beyond, say, ten years the basic uncertainties increase significantly. Yet for some professions, the time span from first choice of occupation to completion of all educational requirements for the profession may be fifteen years or more.[5] Frequent revisions of forecasts to take account of unforeseen developments and hoped-for corrective actions by employers and educational authorities can help to avoid some of the weaknesses in manpower forecasts.

Manpower projections must be judged by their suitability for the purposes they serve. For career choice and vocational guidance, long-run trends and relative magnitudes of change may be satisfactory. Exactness in quantitative terms is unnecessary. For planning of vocational training programs, more detailed data on numbers and on kinds of instruction are desirable. One has to bear in mind that manpower forecasting can serve many useful purposes even when it is only roughly right rather than perfectly correct. With large movements of qualified workers into and out of the labor force during each year,

[5] For a discussion of some of the problems in this and the preceding paragraph see "Meeting of Experts on Employment Forecasting Techniques," Manpower and Social Affairs Directorate, Organization for Economic Cooperation and Development, Paris, France, September 30, 1964, pp. 3-8 (mimeo.).

with a large flow of generally well-educated youth into gainful employment each year, and with the adaptability of much American manpower, forecasts that come anywhere within range may be almost as valuable as those that land right in the bull's eye.

Modifications in Hiring Standards

Americans generally take demand as a given fact. Our predilections are to avoid any questioning of the validity of demand or its component parts. Only since World War II have questions been raised concerning particular aspects or elements of labor demand. Laws have been passed forbidding discrimination in labor demand on grounds of race, sex, or age.[6]

The composition of labor demand is now beginning to be questioned on another score. Many firms, it is claimed, have hiring standards that are too rigid and educational requirements for new employees that are unduly high for most jobs. Although the educational level of the labor force has been rising significantly, the hiring standards of large firms have, generally speaking, risen more rapidly. In 1952 the median (or middle number) of school years completed by the civilian work force 18 years of age or over was 10.9. Twelve years later, in 1964, that figure had risen to 12.2 years. For the unemployed the educational me-

[6] Minimum-wage and maximum-hours laws did not question the composition of demand. Rather, they were concerned with the adequacy of the compensation and the length of the work day or work week.

[117]

dian rose from 10.1 years in 1952 to 10.9 in 1964.[7] High school graduation has been required for new hires in companies that forty years ago did not even insist on an elementary school education. Yet the skill and educational requirements for jobs below the management and professional ranks have not advanced as rapidly as hiring standards. What explains this apparent tendency for hiring standards to outstrip job requirements and gains in educational levels?

A number of developments since the 1920's help to explain the relative rise in hiring standards in certain sections of the economy. They include the high risks and obligations for employers under collective agreements, the shift from hiring for the job to work-life hiring, the use of educational requirements as a proxy for or measure of personal attributes, the ease of management and the work-force flexibility provided by a well-educated work crew, and relatively high levels of unemployment permitting the application of high standards. Brief examination of each of these five factors may help to indicate the kinds of corrective measures that might be appropriate and effective.

Developed in the 1930's as a means of preventing discrimination against union members, two practices have spread widely in manufacturing and other

[7] The median for the jobless in March 1957 was 9.4 years. See *Manpower Report of the President . . . 1965*, U.S. Government Printing Office, Washington, D.C., 1965, Table B-12, p. 226.

industries under collective bargaining. They are (a) seniority (length of service in the unit) as the criterion for rationing employment opportunities and determining the order in which workers are offered the opportunity to qualify for promotion, and (b) a short probationary period (30 to 60 days), after which the new employee has seniority rights and all the protections against disciplinary action that are provided by the grievance procedure, the final step of which generally is arbitration to resolve differences.

Those two practices increase the risk and cost of putting workers on the payroll. After the probationary period, it is difficult to eliminate an employee who turns out to be of relatively poor quality, and his seniority may place him ahead of many able employees in the queue for opportunity to move up the promotional ladder. In other words, not only must a management live with any hiring mistakes that are not discovered and corrected quite soon, but also some of those less qualified may have top priority in the bidding for promotion—a good case must be presented to deny them promotion. In addition, the costs of recruitment, selection, indoctrination, and training of new employees have increased considerably, so that the company has a significant investment in an employee by the time the probationary period expires. Now that unions and grievance procedures are well entrenched and enjoy legal protections, there may be a case for a longer probationary or testing period for a certain number or percentage of new hires who may not seem to meet a particular standard at the time they apply for employment. That might encourage employers to take more risks with persons whose educational records have deficiencies but who may seem to have potentialities.

Seniority and the development costs for new employees have tended to extend greatly the horizon of American management with respect to employment policies, especially in larger, well-established firms. Instead of hiring for a particular job, they may select and employ persons in terms of a potential work career in that firm. New hires come in at the bottom rung of a promotion ladder and advance occupationally by order of seniority, with the aid of on-the-job training for positions that may be, to a significant extent, peculiar to that firm or industry. Recruitment and selection of new employees is not in terms of their qualities for the entrance job (which may be a strong-back type like yard labor) but for jobs up the promotion ladder. In short, people are hired for some kind of average sequence of jobs envisioned for a work career in the company. That conception of employment helps to explain the rise in hiring standards, especially educational requirements, in firms where seniority and promotion from within is the general practice.

To some extent, school records may serve as a measure of the attributes that are stressed in work-career hiring and employment. Those attributes are personal characteristics such as stability, diligence, discipline, adaptability, ambition, and perseverance. Persons who complete high school or some other educational or training program with good records of attendance and progress seem likely to make a similar record in the work place. In the absence of good tests for determining such personal attributes, employers may use school records as a proxy for test scores.

A uniformly high quality of work force eases the problems of management. High intake standards facilitate flexibility of use. With seniority governing transfer and promotional opportunities, the problem of repeatedly matching men and jobs is less difficult if all have a good educational background and a fairly high capacity for learning and adaptation. Such a work force helps to minimize the costs of "bumping" and on-the-job training when employment in the firm has to be reduced.

The relatively high rates of unemployment in the United States since 1953 have presented employers with an abundant supply of labor from which to choose. Thus, managements have been able to maintain high hiring standards and to employ people who, for many years at least, are overeducated for their jobs. Adopting a policy of work-career employment, companies may prefer male workers in their early twenties who are married and, therefore, ready to settle down and pursue a work career in one company. Managements may hesitate to invest in the development of younger workers because of their high turnover rates, or in older workers because of their limited adaptability and because the pay-off period for the investment in their development is shorter.

During the past three decades in the United States a distinct pattern of employment has developed and spread until it now predominates. It is the pattern of work-career employment and strong ties to the firm, achieved by such means as seniority and promotion rights, insurance benefits of various kinds including medical care and pensions, vacation rights, and additional privileges and other forms of compensation. All of them are tied directly and solely to continued employment with that firm. The company becomes a self-contained mobility unit, with ports of entry only at the bottom of seniority units or promotion ladders, except in the case of professional, managerial, or white-collar positions that require completion of special preemployment training.

The traditional labor market, with jobs opening up to outsiders at practically all occupational levels and with few barriers to movement laterally between firms, still prevails in much small-scale business. That is the general situation, for example, in agriculture, service industries, and highly organized lines without seniority and with industry-wide or market-wide benefit arrangements, such as building construction, the needle trades, and longshoring. However, the pattern of work-life employment in a company is typical of large and medium-sized firms, whether they are unionized or not, and firms with 300 or more employees account for over half of all private employment.

For the most part, large firms have better supervision, better training programs, and better-developed ladders of promotion than small firms do. Therefore, they should be in a good position to experiment with some new hires who fail to meet their high hiring standards, especially if the probation or trial period could be extended in such cases. In 1964 and 1965, companies in life insurance and other industries experimented with hiring school drop-outs. Many of those youths developed into quite satisfactory employees. More such experimentation with relaxing stiff hiring standards is needed if the United States is to avoid separation of the economy into high-hiring-standard and low-living-standard sections. It may, for example, be convenient but certainly is unnecessary, in view of the job requirements and the high labor turnover, for all telephone operators or insurance clerks to be high school graduates.

One of the reasons high hiring standards are so troublesome is because this country has not built enough bridges between school and normal work or adequate bridges outside business firms for a person who wants a "second chance" to develop a new work career. As explained in Chapter 3, a significant element in such bridging is supplied by the Employment Service in some European countries. The next chapter explains how apprenticeship programs can provide school-industry bridges for youth, and how training programs can furnish "second chance" opportunities for adults. In one way or another, the try-out periods for European youth in industry tend to be much longer than is the case in the United States.

Company hiring standards should be reexamined in the light of European experience and the results of recent experiments in this country. More experimentation and research are needed with respect to relaxation of high hiring standards for some school drop-outs and disadvantaged youths who have possibilities of becoming quite satisfactory employees under good supervision. Also, probationary periods specified in collective agreements should be lengthened for selected youths for whom management is willing to risk some lowering of hiring standards.

Job Creation for Special Needs

To the extent that unemployment is due to a general condition of sluggish demand, aggregative measures such as monetary and fiscal policy are the appropriate methods of attack. However, monetary-fiscal action cannot correct certain types of structural deficiency. In those cases, pumping up aggregate demand may result, for the most part, in higher prices.

Americans are prone to assume that, where effective demand for a good or service exists, private enterprise will find a way to fill it. We are not accustomed to thinking of government assistance in the organizing of effective arrangements to meet scattered demands. One exception is in agriculture where the Federal-State Employment Service does schedule workers and transportation so as to meet scattered demands for both local and migrant labor.

The feasibility of a somewhat similar arrangement

for meeting the scattered demands of householders for repair and maintenance services should be seriously considered. Because of the lack of readily available commercial arrangements, householders often either themselves perform or buy only in the most minimal amounts or postpone for at least a period of time such work as the following: repairing household appliances (radios, televisions, washers, driers, toasters, and stoves), painting the dwelling inside or outside, wallpapering, correcting minor plumbing defects or inconveniences, making minor carpenter repairs, washing windows, waxing and refinishing floors, gardening, and caring for the lawn and trees.

Failure to fulfill effective demand quickly may often mean postponement of employment or stillbirth of a job. The net number of jobs in the country that could be created by proper arrangements for meeting such service demands is difficult to estimate. Partly, of course, the existing price or the quality of service may discourage demand, but partly it is the absence of sufficient and easily available "visible" supply, if householders' statements have any validity. Some intermediary arrangements are needed to bring together the supply of jobless workers (mainly in cities) and the household service demand (heavily in the suburbs) under appropriate conditions.

A basic question is whether a decentralized program to provide organization, training, supervision, and financial and other responsibility would be able to fulfill much more of the demand at existing or lower prices. Temporary-help firms like Manpower, Inc. and

Kelly Girls developed to provide stenographic service for employers when the Employment Service did not supply such intermediary facilities. This required capital, promotional activities, a hiring program, billing and accounting facilities, and responsibility for results—in short, entrepreneurship.

The same entrepreneurship would be needed for clearing agencies to meet householders' service needs.[8] Also, assurance of good moral character and reliability would be essential for people employed in and around the home. For much of the work, however, the educational requirements would be low, and the special training period for the bulk of the workers could be quite short. That would be true, for example, of care of the lawn, window-washing, and floor-waxing; also, those services could be performed by workers with minor handicaps or disadvantages.

This discussion of arrangements for job creation in the household services area illustrates the applicability of manpower planning in all sectors of the economy. The service area has been expanding and promises to expand at a more rapid rate in the future, yet service workers have persistently had relatively high unemployment rates. Preparation for future expansion should involve much more than the conventional types of employment exchange and vocational training or retraining. Planning for the manpower re-

[8] For a realistic discussion of these problems see "Report of the National Manpower Policy Task Force: Programs and Policies of Job Creation," Washington, D.C., June 1965, 26 pp. (mimeo.).

quirements of the service field necessitates coordination of such various activities and agencies as urban transportation, the Small Business Administration, chambers of commerce, unions, the schools, the poverty program, and the Employment Service. Most of the coordination and activity must be at the local level.

Another area of employment creation is the provision of work for handicapped persons in "sheltered workshops." The role that sheltered workshops can play in employment creation as well as in work training and transition to normal work can be illustrated by the program in Sweden.

Sweden has about 5,000 sheltered workshops ranging in size from 10 to 70 work places. They are operated and supervised by the municipalities and a few foundations. The Employment Service selects the workers for the workshop. Most of them are physically and mentally handicapped persons or workers with troubles that may require medical or psychiatric consultation or care. In many sheltered workshops those workers are mixed with persons who are in a regular vocational training program. The idea is to approach a normal work-training situation (i.e., the simulation of a regular commercial operation) and to avoid segregating the handicapped at work.

Essentially, the workshops are production-training centers. They produce a variety of items, either on commission or for direct sale to stores and other customers. The following list indicates the wide variety of products and activities in which sheltered

workshops specialize, with each workshop concen-
trating on a few items: wooden handicrafts, machinery parts, electrical and electronics parts, stuffed
animals, woven goods, ornaments, plastic maps, and
graphic reproductions; photocopying, offset printing, bookbinding, typing and duplicating letters and
notices, and performing services with computer
equipment.

The workers in the sheltered workshops are paid
according to regular commercial piece rates, with a
minimum guarantee. They are permitted to work only
a half day if that is necessary. Those in the shop under
regular training arrangements receive training allowances. The Labor Market Board subsidizes the operation of the sheltered workshops by paying 50 per
cent of the net costs of their operation (the net losses)
and part of the costs for machinery and other capital
investment.

The sheltered workshops aim to prepare the sheltered workers for regular commercial employment.
When they are sufficiently trained and productive,
their transfer to employment in private industry is
arranged, usually through the Employment Service.
Particular efforts are made to prevent employment
in sheltered workshops from becoming a normal pattern of work life. Not infrequently, workers are transferred between workshops to provide a new environment and to help avoid any tendency to settle in.
And the workshops themselves have the appearance
of, and are operated as, up-to-date businesses in order
to facilitate transfer to regular jobs in industry,

which a remarkably high proportion of the workshop personnel ultimately achieve.[9]

In addition to the sheltered workshops, other types of sheltered work are provided by the national, county, and local governments in Sweden. They include work in museums and libraries, keeping of office records, clearing and cleaning of parks and forest areas, light and simple repair work on public buildings, and light work on streets and roads. Most of this sheltered work is for older workers who are unsuited for retraining for a new line of work. Local authorities receive a 50 per cent subsidy from the Labor Market Board for such sheltered employment.

The United States has not faced up squarely to the problem of employment creation, coupled with training, for the physically, mentally, psychologically, and socially handicapped. A poor alternative to rehabilitation through sheltered employment is the requirement in some countries such as Great Britain, France, Austria, and Western Germany that a certain percentage, say 3 per cent, of the work force of firms of a certain size must consist of persons registered as disabled by the Employment Service, and that certain jobs such as elevator operator be reserved for those so registered.[10] Sheltered workshops are a means of avoiding that kind of compulsion.

[9] In some cases, of course, deterioration in health makes a regular job an impossibility, and sheltered workers have to be discharged from the workshop for health reasons.

[10] Such requirements were stimulated by the need to provide employment for persons disabled in World War II. In addition, Great Britain has Remploy Limited, operating 90

Part of the poverty program in this country involves job creation for disadvantaged persons. But a work-training program for handicapped and less advantaged persons should be established on a broader and more permanent basis. It should, of course, be adapted to American conditions and practices. But above all, it should be a regular and integral part of an over-all program of manpower planning.

Manpower Planning and Employment Creation

In the United States a rather sharp separation has existed at the national level between planning to influence the level of employment and planning for the use of manpower resources. Federal agencies concerned mainly with monetary and fiscal policy (the Council of Economic Advisers, the Treasury, the Federal Reserve Board, and the Budget Bureau) have been deciding national policy with respect to the creation of demand and the general level of employment. On the other hand, the Department of Labor and the Department of Health, Education, and Welfare have dealt chiefly with the supply side—education, training, counseling, and referral for placement.[11]

---

factories which provide sheltered employment to about 9,000 disabled workers under a revenue grant from the Ministry of Labour; Western Germany began in 1963 a program of subsidizing "rehabilitation centers" in addition to providing temporary sheltered employment for about 8,000 handicapped and aged unemployed each year.

[11] As an intermediary agency, the Employment Service can be considered on both sides of the market, but it has no demand-creation functions.

Those agencies dealing with the demand side have tended to think in aggregate terms and to assume that sufficient over-all demand will largely iron out particular imbalances in demand and supply through the working of market forces. Agencies concerned chiefly with the supply side deal primarily with the development and placement of individuals at the local level. They are, therefore, more conscious of the institutional and other barriers to rapid adjustment of supply to changing demand, the human problems of adaptation to innovations, and the limits of market forces alone as means of overcoming labor shortages or oversupply in particular occupations and areas.

One result of this dualism in approach and responsibility has been that little connection has existed each year between the President's *Economic Report* in January and the President's *Manpower Report* in March.[12] The same is true of the Council of Economic Advisers' report dealing with general employment policy under the Employment Act of 1946 and the Secretary of Labor's report on manpower requirements, resources, utilization, and training, which is required under the Manpower Development and Training Act of 1962. Different Congressional committees receive and discuss the Economic and Manpower reports. Thus, at the Executive and Congressional levels, the demand side (employment policy) and the supply side (manpower policy) are not well integrated. That constitutes a serious defect in both

[12] The first annual *Manpower Report of the President* was in 1963.

employment and manpower planning in the United States.

Various administrative arrangements have been proposed to achieve more coordination and integration of employment and manpower planning and policy within the executive branch of the Federal Government and in Congressional consideration of programs. These arrangements include the appointment of an over-all national council for economic affairs that would deal with both employment and manpower policy; the coordination of all economic policy in the Bureau of the Budget; and the appointment of a manpower expert as one of the three members of the Council of Economic Advisers to help expand its analysis and planning in the manpower area.[13]

However, more than a new mechanism at the top is required if meaningful coordination and integration are to occur. Responsibilities also need to be shared. For example, the manpower authorities should be given some powers of demand creation as they have in Sweden. In addition to the sheltered work-

[13] For a statement of these and other proposals, see *Toward Full Employment: Proposals for a Comprehensive Employment and Manpower Policy in the United States*, Report of the Subcommittee on Employment and Manpower of the Committee on Labor and Public Welfare, United States Senate, 88th Congress, 2nd Session, U.S. Government Printing Office, Washington, D.C. 1964, pp. 44-45. See also Frederick H. Harbison, "Critical Issues in American Manpower Policy and Practice," *Proceedings of the Seventeenth Annual Meeting of the Industrial Relations Research Association* (G. G. Somers, ed.), Industrial Relations Research Association, Madison, Wisconsin, 1965, pp. 218-222.

shop and sheltered employment, the Swedish Labor Market Board has three other instruments at its command with which to create new employment opportunities and to combat cyclical declines. Two of them are directed at the employment needs of particular areas: Board financing of emergency public works (especially roads) to reduce seasonal and cyclical unemployment; and Board power to make grants to speed up the letting of public works contracts for labor-market reasons. The third instrument is control of investment reserve funds set aside by private companies, which receive appreciable tax reductions if they use those funds at a time the Board regards as desirable for anti-cyclical purposes.

To achieve meaningful integration of employment and manpower planning and policy it would not be necessary for the manpower authorities in the United States to have all the demand-creating powers granted to the Swedish Labor Market Board. They should, however, have some of them. A small part of the American labor force will need the work-training type of employment provided in sheltered workshops in Sweden. The manpower authorities in this country should have some operating responsibilities on the demand side in order to gain meaningful participation in employment planning and policy. Only when they share in authority for demand creation will an "active manpower policy" be an integral part of national economic policy.

The analysis in this chapter has led to four concrete proposals. The widespread development of work-career hiring standards suggests a reexamination of their blanket application and the need for lengthening of probationary periods for a select group who fail to qualify on all counts. Serious consideration should be given by the manpower authorities to arrangements for job creation in the household services area. Sheltered workshops should be developed locally with Federal financial assistance as a means of preparing handicapped elements in the work force for regular commercial employment. And the manpower authorities should be given some significant operating responsibilities for demand creation to help in the integration of manpower and employment planning and policy. Implementation of those four recommendations would begin to correct some serious weaknesses in the manpower program in this country.

··

CHAPTER 6

Planning Adjustments in Supply

··

MANPOWER planning centers chiefly on the adjustments necessary to adapt labor resources to changing job requirements. Forward planning aims to influence supply in line with projected demand so as to avoid serious imbalances or underutilization of abilities and talents. As previously explained, the means of influencing supply to adjust to forecasted needs include: effective spread of manpower information, career counseling, education and training programs, referral to jobs in accordance with abilities and projected needs, reduction of institutional and other obstacles to job transfer, and wage-benefit levels that encourage needed shifts between industries and occupations. Such measures are supposed to provide proper mobility on the supply side—the matching of manpower requirements and resources by adjusting the resources.

Proper labor mobility is a complex concept with many dimensions. Mobility includes movement[1] between occupations, industries, areas, firms, and jobs within the firm through transfer and promotion. Optimum mobility means mobility that is neither too

---

[1] Strictly speaking, mobility includes potential or threatened movement as well as actual movement. Potential movement can affect relative compensation and thus affect many aspects of labor movement.

little nor too much. Counseling, training, and job-exchange services may be considered mobility-promoting. If properly performed they may also be mobility-reducing. Indeed, low labor turnover has been suggested as a test or aim of successful Employment Service operation. And good manpower planning should result not only in the prevention of shortages and surpluses but also in better fits of men and jobs all up and down the line and, therefore, less dissatisfaction.

In an economy characterized by great changes in technology and jobs, flexibility in the labor force is highly desirable. General education and training help to increase occupational flexibility. Flexibility in the use of labor is reduced, on the other hand, by racial and sex discrimination and by social barriers to fluidity in the nation's labor force. High hiring standards and specialized training requirements, especially if a long training period is necessary to meet them, of course also reduce fluidity of the work force. It is noteworthy that an appraisal of unfilled orders of the Federal-State Employment Service at the end of 1964 showed that most of them were for skills and occupations that had long been in short supply.[2]

The orderly adjustment of supply to demand is complicated by the shift in demand toward more skilled, white-collar, and professional-technical jobs. Those types of employment generally require consid-

[2] V. D. Chavrid and Harold Kuptzin, "Employment Service Operating Data as a Measure of Job Vacancy," *Employment Service Review*, 2 (April 1965), p. 6.

erable education and training, and usually are beyond the reach of disadvantaged groups. Between 1947 and 1964, the white-collar component of the nation's labor force increased from 35 to 44 per cent, and professional and technical workers rose from 6.6 to 12.2 per cent. During the same seventeen year period, farm workers fell from 14 to 6 per cent, and unskilled and semi-skilled blue-collar workers declined from 27.3 to 23.6 per cent of the country's total working population. Those occupational shifts indicate a rising demand for workers with certain educational and social backgrounds.

The problems of planning and preparing supply to meet such shifts in manpower demand are examined in this chapter under the following headings: planning and mobility; education and training; and national interests in supply adjustment. Manpower planning on the supply side is as comprehensive as the economy. Division into separate topics is only for convenient consideration of the parts in relation to the whole.

Planning and Mobility

Adjustment on the supply side has often been analyzed in terms of labor mobility. It has been said that the promotion of mobility should be the main aim of manpower planning and policy. The meaning and implications of that vague generalization must, however, be explored.

Labor mobility, as already explained, is a multidimensional concept. It has time, space, personal, skill, and incentive aspects. And a single movement by a worker may involve change of employer, of occupation, of industry, and of geographic location. Mobility may be either forced or voluntary. In a normal year, as much movement from one employer to (ultimately) another employer is likely to result from forced change through lay-off, discharge, or job termination as from voluntary quits in hopes of gain. And the gross movement during a year is many times the net change at the end of the year.

The net differences between projected requirements and qualified resources over, say, a ten-year period could provide a conceptual measuring rod for judging desirable and undesirable mobility and for guiding efforts to influence labor mobility. Indeed, the development of a set of mobility guidelines would represent a significant step forward in manpower planning and policy. The guidelines would, of course, need to be applied under a program of "more and better information on employment opportunities in job market areas throughout the country,"[3] and in connection with a much more adequate program of counseling for youths (as explained in Chapter 3) and for adults, much more effective interarea arrangements for clearance of jobs and qualified job-seekers, and more suitable programs for developing qualified labor for a wide range of occupational categories.

In the absence of such guidelines, much labor

[3] *Manpower Report of the President . . . 1965*, U.S. Government Printing Office, Washington, D.C., 1965, p. 146.

mobility is uninformed or misdirected, and thus un-economic and wasteful. Generally, of course, it is the better informed, the better educated, and the young who are the most mobile. The unskilled and semi-skilled, the less educated, and the older workers are least likely to move geographically or occupational-ly. Usually they are the ones with the least access to information about employment opportunities else-where and the least resources for moving to another area or for preparing themselves for another occupa-tion. A comparison of 10 Standard Metropolitan Areas with high unemployment and 10 with low unemployment shows that between 1955 and 1960 the 10 relatively depressed areas lost 3 per cent of their employed men and the 10 relatively prosperous areas gained 3 per cent through migration. The net losses and gains were in the right direction in 17 of the 20 areas. However, in-migration into the de-pressed areas was more than two and a half times the net loss, and out-migration from the prosperous areas was almost triple the net gain. Indeed, the gross flow of out-migrants was higher in the prosperous areas (11.6 per cent) than in the depressed areas (9.0 per cent).[4]

The development of a set of mobility guidelines would be difficult not only because of the many di-mensions of labor mobility but also because of differ-ences among national, local, and employer interests in labor mobility. The mobility guidelines would have to include the outlook for different occupations, indus-

[4] See *Ibid.*, pp. 152-153.

tries, and areas and regions. They would have to deal with such outlooks in terms of different characteristics of persons—age, sex, education and training, etc. The guidelines or directions would need to be formulated for, say, the next three and ten years. Too short a focus would not be worthwhile for planning purposes.

The mobility guidelines should be broken down into long-run (ten-year) occupational, industry, and geographical guidelines and short-run (one to three years) guidelines. The long-run guidelines would be particularly useful for workers up to, say, age 40. The short-run guidelines would be designed not only for workers 40 years of age and older but also for geographic movement of young workers and adults of all ages who could improve their earnings merely by geographic movement or by brief training in combination with such movement.

Some concrete material may help to illustrate the usefulness of mobility guidelines. The long-run occupational and industry guidelines could, for instance, be based mainly on the data prepared by the Bureau of Labor Statistics for the *Occupational Outlook Handbook*. They could indicate those occupations that are forecast to be in short supply over the next decade (the specific professional, technical, skilled, service, and white-collar occupations) and the occupations and industries of long-run decline, such as coal mining, the railroad trades, farm work, and unskilled and semi-skilled work. The same could be done for geographical areas in which employment growth is projected to increase over the next decade at various rates above the national average and those with differing rates of relative or absolute decline, such as coal mining areas, regions of resource exhaustion, railroad-shop centers, regions of declining agricultural employment, and so forth. Of course, economic growth in some economically distressed areas, such as the Appalachian Region, may experience significant economic expansion under the stimulus of Federal programs, but the types of job opportunities that would expand and their general rate of expansion over the next decade can be estimated. All this sort of material the guidelines would point up for general public use.

Differences of view with respect to desirable mobility may exist among the national government, localities, and employers. The Federal Government is interested in nationwide matching of supply to demand and sufficient occupational and geographic mobility to achieve that purpose. A community or an employer may have rather parochial interests and be concerned with special local problems. For instance, a community may have little interest in training for some of the professions because its leaders know that, with a nationwide market for such occupations, the community would be likely to lose many of the graduates. An employer who is able to select employees according to high hiring standards may have little interest in persons in the nation's work force who are well below his hiring qualifications. Differences of viewpoint and interest frequently arise concerning the type of education and vocational training to be supplied locally and concerning which kinds of training, and what amounts, should be financed by employers, the local school district, the State, and the Federal Government.

If at the outset the mobility guidelines were drawn in rather broad terms, such differences of interest might present few serious conflicts or problems. With experience, research, and the accumulation of more information, the Federal Government would be in a position to refine the guidelines and make them more specific and detailed.

The development of mobility guidelines would have many advantages. The guidelines would necessitate sharp delineation of desirable and undesirable kinds of mobility. They would raise questions about the most effective means for encouraging mobility and maintaining immobility so as to improve manpower development and worker-job matching, judged from a broad viewpoint and a fairly long perspective. Furthermore, mobility guidelines would stimulate new thinking on old problems within the Federal-State Employment Service, and would focus upon the specific application and widespread use of available data.

Promotion of mobility has been referred to as the major aim of manpower planning. Therefore, before discussing obstacles to mobility and some of the means of facilitating adaptability of the nation's work force, some remarks on the circumstances under which immobility should be encouraged would seem to be in order.

As explained in Chapter 2, some labor mobility can have fairly high individual and social costs. When an employee has accumulated a considerable length of service with a firm, both the employer and the worker may have large sunk costs that would be lost with change of employer. That would be especially true if the change of employer also involved shift of occupation and residence. The individual and social cost of change of employers is greater the longer the seniority, the older the employee, and the larger the special value he has for the present employer. In addition, there are benefits to the individual and society when a worker has gotten on a ladder of promotion in a firm and the upper rungs of the ladder will make good use of his potential abilities. Also, reduced labor turnover can cut down on employer costs, worker costs, and loss of potential production. A certain amount of job-shopping and diversity of experience, especially for youth, may serve an educational purpose, but some turnover certainly is needless and wasteful and could be avoided by proper information, testing, and counseling.

Since mobility may or may not be beneficial, depending on the circumstances, barriers to mobility likewise may serve useful purposes and yet may also obstruct adjustment and the best utilization of the nation's labor resources.

In various ways, parts of the nation's work force may become "locked in" their present jobs or present localities when a change, if transfer costs were not made so high by various barriers, would be to the worker's comparative advantage and would increase the nation's Gross National Product. That is the case, for example, when a worker has acquired considerable seniority, vacation, and benefit rights that would be lost with change of employer, yet his talents could be put to more productive use with other employers. In that case the barriers are the accumulated rights that are tied to continued employment with the present firm.

Another type of "lock in" occurs among unemployed and underemployed workers with poor education and little skill who reside in areas of declining employment opportunity for them. They lack the job information, the interarea connections, and the resources to finance preparation for a new start and moving costs.

The barriers to mobility may also take the form of exclusions that tend to balkanize the labor force. Certain groups may be "locked out" of job opportunities by racial or sex discrimination in hiring or promotion, or by other barriers in employer hiring practices. For instance, separate company recruiting offices or separate public employment offices for blue-collar and white-collar workers may tend to prevent the blue-collar worker with white-collar potential from being considered for, and employed in, a white-collar job.

The structure of compensation (wages and fringe benefits) may also be a barrier to movement out of labor-surplus and into labor-shortage industries and occupations. In large sections of the economy, wage-benefit levels are the reverse of what they should be for labor mobility purposes. They are high for un-skilled and semi-skilled workers in mass-production industries, mining, and railroading, in which such employment has been declining, and relatively low in expanding service lines like schools, hospitals, and hotels and restaurants.

Wage structures seem to be rather insensitive to changing manpower needs. A study of wages and mobility in this country and abroad by a nine-man team of experts, published by the Organization for Economic Cooperation and Development in 1965, found that "over the last ten or fifteen years, changes in earnings differentials have not in practice been a factor of major importance in the big shifts that have taken place in employment between industries, oc-cupations and regions."[5] They found that, despite marked shifts in employment between industries and occupational groupings, wages (measured by earn-ings) rose at approximately the same rate in different sectors of the economy. Expanding industries were able to acquire and hold the workers they needed without raising their wage levels vis-à-vis the rest

[5] See summary, "Wages and Labour Mobility: A New Step Forward in Incomes Policy," *The OECD Observer*, No. 16 (June 1965), p. 4. The title of the full report is *Wages and Labour Mobility*, Organization for Economic Cooperation and Development, Paris, France, 1965.

For a study of the United States data that comes to similar conclusions see Lloyd Ulman, "Labor Mobility and the In-dustrial Wage Structure in the Postwar United States," *Quarterly Journal of Economics*, 79 (February 1965), pp. 77-94.

of the economy. Thus, the role that wage relationships did play in allocating labor turned out "on actual examination to be weaker than one might expect."[6]

Current interfirm and interarea differentials in wage rates might be thought by some to be adequate guides for labor mobility. The discussion in this chapter and in Chapter 2 indicates that this would be the case only under a special set of circumstances. It assumes the proper flexibility in wage structures, a knowledge of employment prospects, and the employment of workers on a short-term basis according to their preemployment qualifications for one particular type of employment. The last, for example, would be the case in a good part of the building trades, the needle trades, and migratory or casual work, all of which have no seniority protections, little in the way of on-the-job training arrangements, and few promotion ladders for adult workers except into management.

If one allows for joblessness accompanied by continuing job vacancies, mobility guidelines would need to take account of the elements of unemployment risk as well as the possibilities for occupational promotion. Under such circumstances, workers might be encouraged to move away from high-wage and high-benefit but declining industries or areas toward expanding service lines, which generally are relatively low in pay and benefits. The longer the employment perspective, the more economic sense it makes to

[6] *Ibid.*, p. 5.

encourage such mobility that is seemingly contrary to the current market signals.

A believer in the operating effectiveness of market criteria might ask why government guidelines for labor mobility are necessary. Why not simply rely on individual workers and individual firms to pursue their own best interests as they see them?

For one thing, it is not possible to obtain adequate, intelligent guidance from current market indicators even if they are supplemented by unemployment information. Such data need to be interpreted and expanded, and the whole bundle should be put in proper perspective. The guidelines would provide proper stress on the long-run interests of individuals and on national interests as well as local interests. They would focus analysis on the different patterns of labor mobility and the two different types of employment world—the casual and craft short-run type and that of the medium-sized and large firms that tend to have long employment horizons and to be complete mobility units within themselves.[7] Firms of any size tend to expand by promoting their existing work force and drawing workers from outside to fill the lower-paying jobs thus vacated. In that way, managements are generally able to acquire new employees without creating larger wage differences between firms than existed before the interfirm shifts in labor

[7] For a further discussion of the implications of such differences see R. A. Lester, "The Structure and Organization of the Labor Market," in *Proceedings of a Symposium on Employment*, sponsored by the American Bankers Association, February 24, 1964, pp. 28-41.

demand. Much of the adjustment to labor shortages is, thus, through labor mobility within the plant or company and by labor mobility into and out of unemployment or the labor force rather than by means of significant alterations in wage structure of the firm or the community or the industry.[8]

It has been claimed that relatively high wage levels for unskilled labor in this country have been an important factor in the high rate of joblessness among youths and poorly educated adults since 1957. The fact that scales for youths from 15 to 21 years of age are significantly below adult rates in Great Britain has been cited as one reason for the low unemployment rate among British youth.

Legal minimum wages probably have caused some relative increase in the prices of certain services with elastic demand (such as work in and around the home and laundering and dry cleaning) and thus could be considered responsible for small amounts of employment curtailment. However, minimums under the Fair Labor Standards Act did not rise any more rapidly between 1949 (when the minimum went to 75 cents) and 1963 (when it went to $1.25) than the average hourly earnings in manufacturing. Minimums have little effect on employment in firms

[8] See R. A. Lester, *Adjustments to Labor Shortages, Management Practices and Institutional Controls in an Area of Expanding Employment*, Industrial Relations Section, Princeton University, 1955; and Ynge Åberg, "The Relationship between Wage and Employment Changes in Individual Firms," *The Swedish Journal of Economics*, 67 (June 1965), especially p. 123.

that hire in at the bottom on a work-career basis, for with them the main cost consideration is work-life compensation. A study of job-finding in an area of high unemployment found that workers who set a wage floor below which they would not accept employment did not tend to be unemployed longer than those who sought work without any minimum reserve wage.[9]

This is not the place to discuss in detail the British wage structure and its relation to British unemployment. However, a few facts will indicate that the age-graded pay scales are less employment-promoting for untrained youth than they might superficially seem to be. First, the wage differences between unskilled and skilled workers in Great Britain are, generally speaking, much smaller in percentage terms than in the United States.[10] Second, for male workers the lower-age scales apply for apprenticeship and other work-training types of employment; where teenagers fill

[9] See *Manpower Research and Training under the Manpower Development and Training Act of 1962, Report of the Secretary of Labor,* U.S. Government Printing Office, Washington, D.C., 1965, p. 131, which summarizes preliminary results from *The Search for Jobs—A Study of How Blue-Collar and White-Collar Workers Seek Work,* to be published by the W. E. Upjohn Institute for Employment Research of Kalamazoo, Michigan.

[10] The actual differentials in earnings may not be as compressed as the negotiated rates for skilled and unskilled might imply. Although there is a tendency in the northern part of Great Britain to pay the minimum rates, in the south the pay of the skilled workers is likely to be above the skilled minimum, and above-minimum rates are more prevalent for skilled than for unskilled workers.

regular unskilled jobs they receive the regular adult rate—the unions insist on it. The tradition in Britain is strong that male youths should not have regular adult jobs until age 21, and that before then they should be receiving some sort of training for their lifetime work.[11] Third, in 1965 many small firms with a few employees were disregarding the graded scale and were paying teenagers the adult rate for jobs that were supposed to have some training component, and some large firms were paying a significantly higher percentage of their 19- and 20-year-old male employees the adult rate. Fourth, in factory work, girls at age 18 are generally paid the adult rate; training for lifetime work is less stressed for them, and they begin to pay the maximum health insurance contribution at that age. Nevertheless, the extent to which age-graded scales have been maintained in Britain in the midst of general manpower shortage and the factors that have permitted tradi-

---

[11] Managements of large companies in Britain state that if they paid adult rates to male teenagers other large firms would follow suit so that any differential recruiting gain would soon be lost. So firm has been the tradition of age-graded scales and so strong the belief in the futility of breaking ranks that, in the midst of a general labor shortage in the London area in 1964 and 1965, one of the large oil companies continued to hire and expand to more than one-fifth of its work force adult West Indians of such low quality that they were considered absolutely unpromotable, rather than employ 16-to-19-year-old males of much higher quality at the regular unskilled rates being paid for the new workers of such low quality.

tion to prevail over market forces would make an interesting and instructive study.

Other barriers to labor mobility are the costs of training and of change of geographic location. Studies show that geographic mobility increases with education and training and that the up-grading of occupational skills through retraining may be an important factor in any relocation program. Where the government supplies the training free, the chief cost of training to the individual is the potential earnings foregone during the training period. Training is discussed more fully in the next section.

A significant barrier may be the costs of movement to another community where employment prospects are better or where a specific job vacancy has been lined up. Those costs include the expenses of personal transportation and of moving household goods, the loss of earnings while moving and any loss on the sale of a home, and the disadvantages of living in a new location. Appropriations under the 1963 amendments to the Manpower Development and Training Act have provided funds for a number of experimental projects to explore the usefulness in this country of governmental financial aid to qualified workers for moving to jobs in other areas where the demand for their skills is strong.

A program of travel and moving grants has been in effect in Great Britain for over two decades and in Sweden since 1957. In Great Britain in the 1962-64 period, the number assisted was about 3,000 or 4,000 a year. In Sweden, where the labor force is one-fifth the size of the British labor force, some 10,000 a year (one-fifth of one per cent of the labor force) have been receiving allowances to help meet the travel and personal and household moving costs involved in relocating from an area of manpower surplus to a new workplace. There is even an indemnity for the need to live temporarily in a hotel in the new location because of housing shortages. Actually, the major obstacle to geographic mobility of labor in Sweden has been the housing shortage. The Swedish financial incentives have proved substantial enough to be an effective inducement for workers to leave unemployment areas in order to seek and accept jobs elsewhere. About one-third of those from the northern part of Sweden who took such allowances to go to the southern part have, however, drifted back to the north. Such return is permissible under the program, for the worker does not commit himself to stay.

Labor mobility can be facilitated by actions that lower or remove such barriers as those just discussed. Often a combination of activities is more effective than a single action as a stimulus to occupational or geographic mobility. For example, job information, vocational guidance, and training tend to be mutually reinforcing. The same is true of manpower information, the elimination of racial discrimination, and a better balanced wage-benefit structure.

In view of the complexity of mobility influences, the development and use of mobility guidelines obviously should be experimental in nature. There should be no assumption of omniscience at the national level. Rather, much reliance should be placed on the market and on the individual decisions of management, workers, and their unions. Persons should be made conscious of manpower needs, employment opportunities, and paths to occupational progress. Government should rely on individual persuasion through information and financial incentives to bring about planning and preparation for personal advancement. In a democracy and an enterprise economy, the effective distribution and use of knowledge is a basic instrument of planning and policy.

Education and Training

The mobility and productivity of a nation's work force are improved by education and training. General education creates better-informed and more adaptable people. It provides the basis for further training or retraining and puts workers in a position to take advantage of developing job opportunities in an increasingly advanced, technological age. Education and training not only develop valuable abilities and skills but they also prepare for the effective utilization of talent resources in the economy.

For the individual, the firm, the community, and the nation, training for work involves forward planning. Investment in education and training is based on a set of assumptions about the future. And the period of advanced planning and preparation lengthens as the economy places more stress on types of employment that require long periods of training, such as professional, technical, and highly skilled work. For example, between 1948 and 1964 total employment in professional and technical positions more than doubled.

Programs of education and training need to be based on the best possible set of assumptions about the future. Especially important is careful forecasting of the demand for university and technical school graduates and the probable supply and rates of new supply in each category. In many lines some substitution is possible, for example, the use of a higher ratio of technicians to scientists and engineers. Also, a part of the existing stock of engineers is employed in non-engineering activities such as sales, personnel administration, and general management. Stocks of trained manpower in non-professional use or currently underutilized provide latitude in manpower planning. Such latitude should be taken into account in training plans, and forecasts of imbalance in requirements and resources need to provide a range of probabilities that allow for the substitution possibilities.

From the viewpoint of manpower planning, education and training programs should be designed to serve a number of purposes. First, they should aim to provide the general and special training for the professions. The demand for the professions has been rising rapidly in the past two decades and promises to continue to rise, even at an accelerated rate in some lines, over the next two decades. Second, there is need for training facilities for white-collar occupations with much shorter periods of special training, a number of which (like stenographer, practical nurse, laboratory technician, and draftsman) seem to have been in relatively short supply for some years in most advanced countries. Third, more adequate and accelerated training for the skilled manual trades is needed than is currently provided by apprenticeship schemes, and more work-study programs are needed to facilitate the transition from school to work. Fourth, ready access to refresher and retraining programs is necessary to remedy skill obsolescence in an economy of rapidly changing job requirements. Fifth, training is necessary for the educationally disadvantaged, especially if they are frequently jobless. Basic education and vocational training serve not only to qualify people for jobs but also to raise aspirations and self-respect, to lower barriers to hiring and advancement and to increase the range of a person's employment possibilities. Sixth, in-service or on-the-job training is needed to adapt individuals to the special requirements of jobs in particular workplaces and to prepare them for promotion. Estimates of the total amount spent each year by industry for on-the-job training vary widely.[12]

A statement of the purposes that can be served by

[12] See, for example, Jacob Mincer, "On-the-Job Training: Costs, Returns, and Some Implications," *Journal of Political Economy*, 70 (October 1962, Supplement), pp. 51-63; and Fritz Machlup, *The Production and Distribution of Knowledge in the United States*, Princeton University Press, Princeton, N.J., 1962, pp. 57-64.

education and training programs raises basic issues concerning their role in manpower planning. Because they can contribute in many different ways to mobility of the labor force, there are different views on the best use of education and training resources in a manpower program. Those who stress the disadvantages of unskilled youth in today's and tomorrow's job markets are likely to emphasize vocational and technical school courses geared closely to forecasted demand. Those who take a longer view may stress a minimum level of basic education and downgrade training or retraining programs that are focussed on immediate job requirements. The requirements, they say, are likely to change, leaving the trained or retrained worker with obsolete skills and insufficient general education to be quickly trained for developing job requirements. And those who stress that workers will have to change occupations two or three times in their work lives are likely to emphasize the need for second-chance opportunities for adults, multiple occupation types of training, and in-service training aimed at developing new skills. Those who wish to build more bridges between school and work will stress work-study programs and a larger mixture of classroom training (including textbooks) in apprenticeship programs.

An obstacle to the redirection of vocational education is, of course, the location and staff of existing training facilities. For instance, in rural areas vocational training in public schools has been largely or exclusively in agriculture. As a result, a third of all

Federally aided, vocational education classes in 1963, outside of home economics, were agricultural classes. Because farm employment has declined sharply since World War II and will continue to do so, such a high proportion makes little economic sense except where the farm training includes preparation for such employment as gardening, landscaping, and farm machinery repair and selling. The movement of population, especially of young people, from rural areas to urban communities has found them largely untrained for the nonfarm occupations available in metropolitan areas. Various studies analyzing the employment of former vocational agriculture students between 1918 and 1960 show that, at the time the studies were made, only about one-third of those former students were employed in farming and an additional one-twelfth in farm-related occupations.[13] The lack of diversified training facilities in rural areas and small towns means that youngsters living in those areas are offered only narrow occupational training opportunities and face difficult problems of occupational choice and adjustment.

The training component of manpower planning poses a number of basic issues. One is the training perspective and content—the extent to which stress should be placed on basic education and preparation

[13] *Manpower Report of the President . . . 1965*, p. 104. The Vocational Education Act of 1963 is helping to correct this agricultural training imbalance by permitting vocational agriculture funds to be used for agriculture-related occupations such as those mentioned in the text.

[157]

for a person's whole work life as opposed to a short-run stress on specialized training geared to immediate jobs that may have poor long-run promise. The second is the allocation of training resources among different elements of the labor force—the young and the old, the talented and the retarded, the employed and the unemployed; persons who select careers requiring long training periods and those who lack elementary language and mathematical skills. Some argue that training under manpower planning should concentrate heavily on the shortage-prone professional, managerial, and technical occupations near the top of the job hierarchy and, at the other end, on the disadvantaged persons who are uneducated and discriminated against so that they are threatened with repeated unemployment and poverty that breeds poverty in the succeeding generation. A third basic issue is the amount of the nation's total resources that should be devoted to education and training for work. This question of the size of the program, or the relative economic value of investment in training, is discussed in the next chapter.

The issue of training perspective has come to the fore in connection with the training projects under the Manpower Development and Training Act. This is not the place for a review and evaluation of that particular training program. Pertinent to the issue are, however, the constraints under which the program has operated. The three limits that have favored short-term training for immediate needs in the vicinity are: (1) There must be reasonable expectation of employment in the occupation for which training is provided, and, in the selection of projects, priority is given to training for skills needed, first, within the local labor market area and, second, within the State. (2) Priority for training is given to unemployed or underemployed persons who cannot reasonably be expected to secure appropriate full-time employment without training. (3) Training allowances for support of trainees and their dependents during training can be paid to a person for a period no longer than 52 weeks, which, under the 1963 amendments, can be extended up to an additional 20 weeks for a person needing basic educational preparation as a prerequisite to taking occupational training.

Undoubtedly, some training under the Manpower Development and Training Act has been too narrowly conceived. Critics have pointed out that retraining programs in this country have overemphasized fulfillment of current demand in the locality as opposed to broader regional and national needs, and have been excessively oriented toward mitigation of unemployment rather than toward long-run development of the individual and promotion of the growth of the economy.[14]

[14] See *OECD Reviews of Manpower and Social Policies: Manpower Policy and Programs in the United States*, Organization for Economic Cooperation and Development, Paris, 1964, p. 74; and Margaret S. Gordon, *Retraining and Labor Market Adjustment in Western Europe*, Office of Manpower, Automation, and Training, U.S. Department of Labor, Washington, D.C., 1965, pp. 195-203.

An examination of the twenty-four occupations with the largest number of trainees under the Manpower Development and Training Act shows that although many are shortage occupations with good long-run prospects, some clearly are not.[15] Typist and secretary, auto mechanic and body repairman, and licensed practical nurse are high on the list of occupations selected for training, which also includes appliance repairman and data processing equipment operator and repairman among the top twenty-four. However, that group also includes assembler and subassembler, farmer and general farmhand, and janitor. Those occupations seem either technologically vulnerable or subject to sharp decline, or are dead-end types of employment.[16] Partly because of the one-year limit on training allowances, the list is notably weak in the subprofessional categories in the scientific, engineering, and health fields and also in the building, printing, and metal trades,[17] where union objections to accelerated training, or any training, in the schools is an additional deterrent.

Arrangements for training young men in the skilled

[15] *Education and Training, the Bridge between Man and his Work*, Third Annual Report of the Secretary of Health, Education, and Welfare to the Congress on Training Activities under the Manpower Development and Training Act, April 1, 1965, U.S. Government Printing Office, Washington, D.C., 1965, p. 15.

[16] Farm training could, if directed at the operation and maintenance of advanced equipment, be valuable from a long-range viewpoint.

[17] Machinist and carpenter are among the top twenty-four occupations.

trades in this country are too limited and old-fashioned to meet modern needs. Apprenticeship training consumes three or four years in such relatively simple trades as painter and carpenter. One result is that over three-fifths of the workers employed in skilled trades with apprenticeship programs have never enrolled in any formal training program but instead have learned whatever they know about the occupation through work experience.[18]

A great gulf exists between vocational education in the schools and apprenticeship training or training on the job. A study of apprenticeship in Great Britain, France, West Germany, and the United States finds that apprenticeship in Europe is a nationwide cooperative effort with good connections with the educational system, whereas in the United States apprenticeship has been allowed to atrophy and has only tenuous connections with other public programs of education and training.[19] Under European programs, apprentices are often scheduled for formal classes during part of each week.

In Great Britain each year over a third of the boys entering employment do so as apprentices to a skilled craft; the corresponding figure for the United States

[18] See J. R. Wason, "Apprenticeship Practices Abroad," in *The Role of Apprenticeship in Manpower Development: United States and Western Europe*, Vol. 3 of *Selected Readings in Employment and Manpower*, Subcommittee on Employment and Manpower, Committee on Labor and Public Welfare, U.S. Senate, 88th Congress, 2nd Session, U.S. Government Printing Office, Washington, D.C., 1964, p. 1338.

[19] *Ibid.*, pp. 1276, 1278, and 1279.

is about one-twentieth. Clearly, well-qualified crafts-men in trades like painter, cement mason, and book-binder, could and should be trained within a year and in significant numbers under the Manpower Development and Training Act.

The second basic issue mentioned above (the al-location. of training resources among different ele-ments in the labor force) also involves weighing and balancing long-range and short-range considerations. Investment in training of youth has a much longer pay-off period than investment in workers in their 50's or 60's. The allocation issue also raises questions concerning the relative needs of individuals and their potential contributions to the economy. For example, the most restrictive bottlenecks tend to occur in oc-cupations requiring long training periods, so that training to avoid such bottlenecks may seem highly productive. At the other extreme, unskilled workers who read at less than the eighth-grade level and per-form number skills at lower than the sixth-grade level may have such employment handicaps that they are threatened with hard-core joblessness. For them, a short intensive course in reading and arithmetic, plus some technical training to qualify them at least as "helpers," may pay high returns in terms of net gains for government budgets and net addition to the na-tion's Gross National Product.[20] And the individual

[20] For an interesting report on the problems of training unskilled, Negro workers in a "culture of poverty" see *Train-ing the Hard-Core Unemployed, A Demonstration-Research*

need for special training efforts by government may seem greater for the potential hard-core jobless than for potential professional workers.

Under manpower planning, training programs need to be related to national as well as local needs. For some occupations there is a national or regional market; other occupations with a more limited market may need also to be fitted into the over-all picture on the supply side. The accident of severe limitations on the training facilities and the variety of job opportunities in a locality should not be mirrored in corresponding limitations on training opportunities for all local residents. A broadly conceived program would not rest so heavily on parochial interests and local restrictions as the Manpower Training and Development program has.

At the outset of this retraining program in 1962 it was necessary to rely heavily on local initiative and support. Administratively, decentralization of project development, of trainee selection, and of placement of trainees was the only practical method of operation. But initial administrative and political considerations should not be permitted to establish permanent patterns. With the 1965 amendments, the program is on a more enduring, long-range basis, with the Federal Government paying nine-tenths rather than two-thirds of the cost. It is time, therefore, for a

Project at Virginia State College, Norfolk Division (An Interim Report), U.S. Department of Health, Education, and Welfare, U.S. Government Printing Office, Washington, D.C., 1964.

reexamination of actual training in the light of national needs and the interests of all parts of the economy. In Western Europe, the adult training and retraining programs for workers have been more definitely geared to national considerations on the supply side. In the United States also, allocation of resources for adult-worker training among the various occupational and worker categories should be based to a larger extent on the mobility needs of the whole economy. The development of mobility guidelines would help to give direction to Federal programs for training such as those under the Manpower Development and Training Act and under the Economic Opportunity Act.

National Interests in Supply Adjustment

In manpower planning and its implementation, the balance between national and local interests is a problem that requires frequent review in the light of current and prospective conditions. Management and labor in the workplace and the personnel in the local employment office are close to job and training needs and know intimately the mobility patterns and obstacles in the community. On the other hand they may be hindered in taking corrective action by local pressures and the absence of broad-gauge leadership. They may fail to see the forest for the trees and thus neglect national considerations and interests.

The problem of balance between local and national considerations runs through the relations of the Federal Government and the States and municipalities in many fields—highways, airports, and agriculture as well as general education, vocational training, career guidance, interarea job clearance, and geographic mobility of labor. The balance shifts with changes in economic and social factors such as transportation developments, rural-urban population distribution, and costs of relief and medical care.

In the manpower field, the balance may, from time to time, shift either toward further centralization or toward more decentralization of particular activities. Although there has been a tendency in most European countries toward greater national uniformity in Employment Service operations during the past two decades, that is less true of adult vocational training, and there are a number of examples of decentralization. For instance, in Sweden the National Labor Market Board in the late 1950's delegated more power and gave more leeway to the County Labor Market Boards, and in the early 1960's a number of matters concerning vocational training and guidance were gradually transferred from the National Board of Technical and Vocational Education to the County Labor Market Boards. In Germany in the early 1960's, as mentioned in Chapter 3, more and more of the registration and referral operations for university-trained personnel were transferred from the Central Office for Labor Placement in Frankfort to the nine State offices.

In many countries, public responsibility for adult education and vocational training is widely dispersed.

Of course, responsibility for in-firm or on-the-job training is scattered among hundreds of thousands of independent firms in this country.

Some have argued that the general aims of manpower policy cannot be achieved without considerable coordination of programs for vocational training, vocational guidance, and financial aid for the geographic mobility of labor. It is said that accelerated training and retraining for adults must not only be directed by the Employment Service but must also be under the general supervision of the national government. In support of that position, it is pointed out that centralization facilitates the exchange of information and experience, the application of research, and the economical and rational use of training resources.[21]

An interesting experiment in balancing the training interests of workers, companies, and the national government is being tried by Great Britain under the Industrial Training Act of 1964. The main objectives of the Act are to ensure an adequate supply of properly trained men and women at all levels in industry, to improve the quality and efficiency of industrial training, and to spread the cost of training more evenly among firms. The administration is largely in the hands of industry training boards, appointed by the Minister of Labour, with equal employer and labor

[21] Franz Lenert, "Comparison of National Manpower Policies," Manpower Division, Organization for Economic Cooperation and Development, Paris, France, 1965, pp. 45-46 (mimeo.).

representation, plus a number of public members.

Under this separate-industry scheme, the training board for each industry has the power to prepare estimates of its industry's future requirements for skilled manpower, to recommend standards of training and further schooling associated with training, and to impose a periodic financial levy on employers in the industry and make grants (from both the levy proceeds and funds granted by government) to employers whose training courses are approved by the board. The levy plus the government grant serves to finance the cost of training in the industry, and the combination of employer levy and grants to employers for approved training serves to distribute training costs equitably among employers in the industry. All actions by an industry board are subject to approval or disapproval by the Minister, who also has the power of allocation of government grants to the boards. The Minister has a Central Training Council to advise him on administration of the Act and training questions generally, including the establishment of training standards especially for occupations that cut across industries. He can at any time direct an industry training board to submit proposals and revise proposals, and, if dissatisfied, he can replace the board by appointing new members. By mid-1965, eight industry boards were in operation, and training levy orders were in effect in four industries.

Already serious problems are being encountered. It is proving difficult to draw industry lines and to place each establishment under only one industry board. In industries already under a board, the amount of paper work is mounting, beginning with a complete report of each firm's actual training activities. Questions are arising as to whether training that has value only for that firm and for no others should be eligible for an industry board's grant or credit. Some are arguing that national standards for training should be established, including a heavy school component in the first year of a worker's training and the streamlining of apprenticeship programs, which some union officials strongly resist. It is proving difficult for industry boards to recruit staffs qualified to assess the levy, inspect firms, pay grants where standards are met, and so forth. The Minister needs a staff for making grants to industry boards, a training inspectorate, and tribunals to hear appeals against assessment of the industry levy. One is reminded of the problems of the National Recovery Administration with industry codes in the United States from 1933 to 1935.

In the United States, empowering an industry board to assess a training levy on an industry defined by that board would be of doubtful constitutionality. Yet the levy is central to the industry training program in Britain.

In this country under the Manpower Development and Training Act, additional on-the-job training is eligible for a subsidy, which averages around half of the non-wage costs of training. The programs combine work and instruction at the workplace or at an approved vocational training institution. There is a requirement of a reasonable expectation of subsequent employment for the trainees who would otherwise be unemployed or underemployed. On-the-job training programs were slow to get started because a whole new system of procedures and standards had to be developed, including proof that approved on-the-job training projects would add to, and not displace, existing programs. By the end of 1964, a total of 1,570 projects for 35,000 trainees had been approved.

A program of tax credits for on-the-job training has been proposed as an alternative to the subsidy method under the Manpower Training and Development Act. However, tax credit tends to be a uniform, blanket type of incentive, under which it would be difficult to direct the program in line with developing needs or to raise training standards. The discussion of the industry-board program in Britain indicates some of the complications and difficulties that a tax-credit program for on-the-job training would encounter. Pertinent also is the experience with the tax-offset method, under which employers are granted Federal tax credits for exemptions under State unemployment compensation laws. A subsidy program is more flexible and better adapted to allocation of training resources according to national requirements and changing needs of the economy as a whole.

Those who strongly back government support for on-the-job training point to such advantages as instruction by practitioners on up-to-date equipment and the high ratio (94 per cent) of job placement in the on-the-job program operated under the Manpower Development and Training Act. It is to be expected that, with its management selecting the trainees and administering the training, a firm would retain most of those who complete the training. However, there is growing appreciation of the importance of basic education and basic training in mathematics and technical knowledge in order to provide occupational flexibility. Such "theoretical" education is stressed in many European programs of on-the-job training. Youths now entering the labor force without professional training are likely to need to shift to a new occupation at least two or three times during their working lives. Basic training, occasionally refreshed, facilitates the ease and speed, and reduces the cost, of such occupational conversion.[22]

In a sense the theme of this chapter has been flexibility to achieve balance. In the manpower field there has been a tendency to think and act in a piecemeal fashion, to start new programs for particular groups, and to press for temporary remedies at the expense of long-run solutions. More attention needs to be given to fitting the diverse elements into a rational, over-all framework. That involves planning and guidance at the national level and skillful application and adaptability at the local level.

[22] For a thoughtful discussion of the pros and cons of a tax incentive program for on-the-job training in this country see Stanley Ruttenberg's statement before the Senate Labor Subcommittee on Employment and Manpower in *Daily Labor Report*, No. 177, September 14, 1965, E-1 to E-3.

Over-all planning and general guidance are needed to facilitate the preparation and adjustment of supply to meet developing demand at all levels of the occupational structure throughout the country. The development of a set of mobility guidelines was proposed as an instrument for stimulating comprehensive analysis and for promoting more rational patterns of labor movement. The mobility guidelines would help in carrying through the other major proposal made in the chapter, namely, a reexamination of the whole program of education and training in the light of national mobility requirements over the next decade. In the field of manpower, the parts acquire meaning and significance from the contribution they make to the whole.

....

CHAPTER 7

The Economics of Manpower Planning and Operations

....

MANPOWER PROGRAMS to promote the mutual adjustment of labor supply and job opportunities are of economic benefit to workers, employers, localities, and the whole economy. But that is true of other activities supported by government, such as highways, housing, health, and research.

Governments need a basis of comparison for allocating funds among competing demands. One kind of comparison that can be made is between broad categories—the manpower program as against all other government activities. The result of that comparison presumably influences the size of the entire manpower program in the total of government budgets. A second type of comparison is between different elements within the manpower program. That comparison should influence the allocation of manpower funds among the various functions and activities, such as forecasting, information analysis and distribution, testing, counseling, employer contacts, the matching of applicants and job vacancies, different types of training, sheltered workshops, and job-creation efforts.

For many economic activities, sales are a measure of the value to customers, and rate of return over cost under competitive conditions is a measure of the efficiency of operations. Government revenue, however, comes mainly from taxes rather than sales, and competitive achievement may be a difficult criterion to apply because the government has a natural monopoly or is essentially a subsidized activity with significant social values. Therefore, alternative methods of systematic analysis and measurement are needed as substitutes for market criteria. One of these is benefit-cost analysis, which is examined in this chapter and evaluated as a basis for an "economics" of manpower planning and operations.

Before discussing benefit-cost analysis, a few comparative figures may serve to highlight the need for some rational means to help guide decisions concerning the size of the total manpower program of a country and the distribution of funds among its constituent parts. Because of possible differences of classification, the figures for different countries may not be exactly comparable, but they are certainly valid for broad comparative purposes.

The first comparison is in terms of the total Employment Service personnel engaged in labor placement and vocational guidance. The number of such personnel for every 10,000 persons in the work force was for 1965[1] as follows: 12.5 for Sweden, 7.3 for Germany, and 3.3 for the United States.[2] Stated some-

[1] All figures apply to fiscal years 1964-65 or 1965-66 unless stated otherwise.

[2] The basic data from which these figures were calculated were supplied to the author by the Bundesanstalt für Arbeits-

what differently, there was one employee of the Employment Service in placement or counseling for every 800 workers in Sweden, every 1,434 workers in Germany, and every 3,035 workers in the United States. If the vocational counseling staff is taken separately, for every 100,000 in the work force, Germany had 16 counselors in the Employment Service, Sweden had 5.5 (not including the career counselors in schools), and the United States had the equivalent of about 3 on a full-time basis, or 5 if those performing part-time counseling are counted fully in the counseling category. Clearly, in terms of staff on Employment Service work, the United States is, relatively, far below both Sweden and Germany.

In terms of public expenditures for the training and retraining of adults for jobs, the United States is well ahead of Germany but far behind Sweden. Sweden in 1963 had about 1 per cent of its working population in such training (with a short-term goal of about 2 per cent), whereas the United States in 1964 had around 0.2 per cent in training under the Manpower Development and Training Act.

---

vermittlung und Arbeitslosenversicherung (Germany) and by the National Labor Market Board (Sweden). For the United States they were taken from *The Role and Mission of the Federal-State Employment Service in the American Economy*, Committee on Education and Labor, House of Representatives, 88th Congress, 2nd Session, December 1964, U.S. Government Printing Office, Washington, D.C., 1965, pp. 9-10. The figure for Great Britain is somewhat larger than the 3.3 for the United States, but the calculation is complicated by separation of the Youth Employment Officers from the Employment Service.

Countries can also be compared by size of total expenditure on labor mobility (manpower information, placement, counseling, adult training, and mobility grants). For these purposes, Sweden in 1963 used 1 per cent of all government expenditures, Germany in 1963 used 0.14 per cent, and the United States in fiscal 1964-65 used about 0.2 per cent.[3] In Sweden these expenditures have risen sharply over the past decade, from 36 million kronor in 1955-56 to 126 million in 1960-61 to 285 million in 1965-66, when they were around 1.25 per cent of total expenditures of the national government, or 0.38 per cent of the national income of Sweden.[4] By 1965, Sweden's total expenditures for employment service and other mobility purposes were larger than Germany's total, although Sweden's working population was only one-seventh the size of the German work force.

The Director General of the National Labor Market Board in Sweden has said that it is impossible to state definitely what proportion of a country's resources should be devoted to public manpower activities including retraining. He points out that "the em-

[3] See Bertil Olsson, "The Size of Appropriate Expenditure for a Public Employment Service," International Management Seminar on the Relation of the Public Employment Services to Management in the Recruitment of Personnel, Madrid, Spain, March 23-26, 1965, Organization for Economic Cooperation and Development, Paris, France, p. 7 (mimeo.).

[4] The total expenditures of the National Labor Market Board for 1965-66 including emergency works and unemployment insurance will be around one billion kronor or approximately one per cent of the national income.

ployment service's information on the labor market
and its help in analyzing the job situation of the individual citizen are perhaps the most important forms
of consumer information provided in modern society." Well-organized, specific information is really
"invaluable to the individual worker in solving problems essential to his security and well-being," and the
dissemination of such information is "money well
spent" from the community's point of view. The benefits to the community, employers, and individual
workers resulting from Employment Service efforts
to adjust labor resources to the market, in his view,
warrant large-scale measures aimed at increasing
geographical and occupational mobility.[5]

The rapid increase in Sweden's manpower expenditures and the remarks of the Director General
sharply raise the question as to whether some economic criteria cannot be developed for helping to
shape the size and content of a manpower program.
In recent years a number of attempts have been made
to apply benefit-cost analysis to programs for training
unemployed workers in the United States. In training
it may be somewhat easier to devise measures of benefits and to relate costs to benefits than it is in other
parts of a manpower program, particularly information and counseling. However, the need for economic
guidance is sufficient to warrant an examination of
the application of benefit-cost techniques to the
budgeting of manpower expenditures. Such an ex-

[5] Olsson (see n. 3), pp. 2, 3, and 6.

amination will be attempted under the following headings: benefits and their measurement; uses of benefit-cost analysis; and social values and national interests.

Benefits and Their Measurement

The basic difficulties in benefit-cost analysis as applied to the manpower field center around measurement of the benefits. Cost figures for Employment Service operations are relatively easy to obtain and calculate. The Federal-State Employment Service has for years had each employee except the top staff allocate his or her time each day among the different functions, and average salary figures enable one to calculate total employment costs of performing each function at the local, State, and national levels.

The calculation of benefits is complicated for two main reasons. The first is that the various functions (providing labor-market information, counseling, worker-job matching, training, etc.) may have beneficial effects in five different areas. A function or service may (a) increase the individual worker's money income and his work satisfaction and reduce the costs of his job search; (b) save on the costs to an employer of recruitment and labor turnover and increase labor productivity in his operations; (c) lower social costs in the community and increase the effective utilization of its human resources; (d) improve local, State, and national budgets by reducing expenditures for items like relief and unemployment compensation and by raising tax income; and (e) increase the Gross National Product by such means as improving worker skills and utilization, avoiding and reducing labor shortages, and shortening periods of unemployment.

The second reason the calculation is complicated is that the benefits are so diverse and dispersed that it is difficult to isolate and determine the contribution that each function of the Employment Service makes in each of the five areas over an extended period of time. An individual worker makes use of the Employment Service for a short period of time, and the benefits to him are intangible and involve the avoidance of mistakes as well as positive decisions. Surveys indicate that workers often fail to recall aid given them by the Employment Service, and are not able at a later date to assess the benefits received from the Service. Employment Service information and services are provided free to company managements and therefore do not enter the company's books. The Service may not be identified as the source of ideas affecting management decisions. It may be difficult to determine what difference the Employment Service makes to the State and the nation in unemployment, labor shortages, or labor allocation. Seldom does one attempt to evaluate the benefits derived from avoidance of things that do not happen.

The assessment of the benefits that flow from particular activities of the Service encounters additional difficulties. Some benefits occur as a consequence of a combination of actions (information, testing, and counseling, or counseling, training, and job referral), so that they cannot be parceled out among particular functions. The full effects of a function like counseling or specific training, whose influence can extend over the person's working life, may be most difficult to predict in a changing world. For certain programs, like sheltered work or demand-stimulating training, it may be hard to determine the net expansion in demand for which that program is responsible, or whether demands were met that otherwise would have remained unmet. Similar difficulties confront efforts to evaluate the benefits of improvement in staff training, as managements in private industry know from experience.

Various methods have been proposed for estimating the value of Employment Service functions. One frequent suggestion is to use the dollar amounts that workers and employers would pay for the services or actually do pay private suppliers for such services. Another method is to attempt to estimate the gains that result from the savings for which the Employment Service is assumed to be responsible. A third method is to develop estimates of the increases in workers' income as a result of Employment Service activities. Each of these methods has significant shortcomings.

The dollar amounts that workers and employers say they would pay or actually do pay to private employment agencies are useful in estimating the value of the job-exchange function for certain types of worker. However, this method has two serious handicaps. First, the Employment Service is in operation largely because, as explained in Chapter 2, the market has notable weaknesses as an allocative mechanism for manpower and because private enterprise does not supply the full range of services and probably could not supply some of them economically. A nation-wide Service has advantages, including economies of scale and promotion of national interests, for such activities as manpower planning, information and research, and improvement of geographical mobility. Second, the private agencies skim off the profitable business, leaving the rest for public attention. That means that the public manpower agencies have to handle the hard-to-place elements in the labor force —those who need counseling, training, and other special service and those who have handicaps, are discriminated against, are uninformed, and lack the ability to pay. In those cases, the public Service may have a greater value than would be indicated by the individual fees collected by private agencies.

The growth of private employment agencies would seem to indicate that their service, largely job-exchange in character, is considered valuable to their customers. According to estimates, private fee-charging employment agencies in the United States increased from 2,231 with 4,580 employees in 1948 to 3,892 with 16,783 employees in 1958, and their receipts rose from 31 to 101 million dollars in that decade.[6] In 1964, it was estimated that there were about 4,300 private agencies, employing about 25,000 persons and collecting about 145 million dollars.[7] The fees charged for placement of a client in a $75-a-week job in 1963 ranged from $117 to $234 in twelve states for which data are available.[8] A very high percentage of the private agencies' applicants are women, most of whom are placed in clerical and secretarial jobs. The 1963 figures for California show that women constituted 85 per cent of the placements made by 1,032 private agencies, and that workers paid $9,739,300 and employers paid $6,597,300 in job fees to those agencies. The average fee per placement was $31.40; the average for female teachers was $258 and for male teachers $269.[9]

Such data do provide some basis for rough estimates of the value of the job-exchange function performed by the public Service. They would, of course, need to be supplemented by some sort of

[6] L. P. Adams, "The Public Employment Service," in J. M. Becker (ed.), *In Aid of the Unemployed*, The Johns Hopkins Press, Baltimore, Md., 1965, p. 219.

[7] Testimony of Jack Skeels in *Public Employment Service*, Hearings before the Select Subcommittee on Labor, Committee on Education and Labor, House of Representatives, 88th Congress, 2nd Session, U.S. Government Printing Office, Washington, D.C., 1964, p. 465.

[8] *Ibid.*, p. 475.

[9] Testimony of Paul Little in *ibid.*, pp. 324, 346-347, and 362. Mr. Little points out that in 1962 the cost of the California Employment Service, including information, testing, counseling, and special programs as well as job-exchange activities, averaged only $21.57 per person actually placed.

[181]

estimates of the value of the other functions that the Employment Service provides to its clients.

The second method for evaluating the benefits of the Employment Service is to attempt to estimate the various kinds of savings for which it is responsible. For workers, they include savings in the cost of job search and in time between jobs. The claim is made, for example, that "repeated studies of these [the Service's] referral practices in California show the public service is able to cut the elapsed time of job filling substantially, often by several weeks."[10] For employers there are such savings as lower recruitment costs and lower turnover costs with test-aided and counseled referrals. For the whole economy, there would be any savings that could be ascribed to the Employment Service from reductions in unemployment and from better matching of jobs and labor resources. Such savings would be especially difficult to identify and quantify. Government budgets would be eased by the savings from lower costs of unemployment relief and unemployment compensation. In that connection, one would have to avoid any double counting of the unemployment savings.

Obviously, the savings method has severe limitations. For many items the estimates would necessarily be quite arbitrary. Also, the savings focus would leave out many beneficial consequences of Employment Service activities. For instance, it would be difficult to include within the savings framework the full contribution of manpower planning, informa-

[10] *Ibid.*, p. 325.

tion, counseling, training, and other activities designed to increase workers' capacity to respond to market demands.

The third method, that of using estimates of personal income increases, has been applied chiefly to training activities. Under that method, the benefits are measured by the change in individual's earned income. The change itself is measured either by a comparison of the person's earned income before and after training, or by a comparison of the earned income of persons after their training with the earned income of a statistically selected "control group" of nontrainees.

The benefits to the jobless or underemployed from training or retraining are of two sorts. One is the gain in the amount of an individual's employment; the trainees may be employed more hours a month or year than before their training or than is experienced by a comparable control group. The other is higher pay per hour than before training or than is received by a comparable group of nontrainees. Calculation of the full benefit difference that results from training involves a significant time dimension. Some estimate must be made of the additional employment and added pay over the trainee's remaining work life. That necessitates speculation concerning the jobs he will have compared with those he would have had if he had not undertaken the training.[11] Clearly the kind

[11] Examples of such calculations of the benefits of retraining are contained in G. J. Somers and E. W. Stromsdorfer, "A Benefit-Cost Analysis of Manpower Retraining," in Somers

of training and the advancement possibilities it opens up for the trainee can make a great difference in the estimated benefit.[12]

Recognizing the limitations of each of the three methods, one could use them in some combination. That might mean, for example, the use of private-agency fees for help in estimating the benefits from the job-exchange function, the earnings-increase method for assessing the benefits of training, and the savings method and other estimation devices for attempting to arrive at some figures for benefits not covered by the first two methods. The very process of trying to quantify benefits would direct attention to important questions concerning the nature and distribution of the beneficial results of Employment Service operations and the most effective means of achieving a particular combination of benefits. The difficulties of estimation should not lead to neglect

---

(ed.), *Proceedings of the Seventeenth Annual Meeting of the Industrial Relations Research Association*, December 28 and 29, 1964, Madison, Wisconsin, 1965, pp. 172-185; D. A. Page, "Retraining under the Manpower Development Act: A Cost-Benefit Analysis," in J. D. Montgomery and Arthur Smithies (eds.), *Public Policy*, Vol. 13, Harvard University Press, Cambridge, Massachusetts, 1964, pp. 257-267; M. E. Borus, "A Benefit-Cost Analysis of the Economic Effectiveness of Retraining the Unemployed," *Yale Economic Essays*, 4 (Fall 1964), pp. 370-429; and Borus, "The Cost of Retraining the Hard-Core Unemployed," *Labor Law Journal*, 16 (September 1965), pp. 574-583.

[12] Since training costs are short run while estimated benefits may extend over many years, the latter need to be discounted by some interest rate for comparison with the costs.

of the important contribution that adequate information can make in a society that relies on decentralized decision-making.

Uses of Benefit-Cost Analysis

In economic analysis, revenues are compared with costs to determine whether and to what extent an operation is profitable or economically justified. Since government services are not usually sold in the market, sales at market prices do not provide a good measure of benefits. Nevertheless even in government the proposition generally holds that rational allocation involves some comparison of projected costs and expected benefits. That kind of comparison should come into focus in the preparation of budgets for future periods.

Benefit-cost analysis provides a systematic way of thinking about allocation problems in government.[13] It helps to make explicit the assumptions that underlie budget figures. Benefit-cost comparisons can aid in determining which activities or parts of activities might be more efficiently or effectively performed by private enterprise and which are more appropriately carried out by government. If a government subsidy is considered desirable, benefit-cost analysis can contribute significantly to decisions as to the kind and size of the subsidy. And, as indicated above, it is not

[13] The application of benefit-cost analysis to seven areas of government is illustrated in Robert Dorfman (ed.), *Measuring Benefits of Government Investments*, The Brookings Institution, Washington, D.C., 1965.

necessary to measure all benefits in order to apply benefit-cost analysis in broad terms.

A framework for considering the method of financing the manpower program is also provided by benefit-cost analysis. The operations of the Federal-State Employment Service have, since 1939, been financed by a Federal payroll tax levied on the first $3,000 that the employer pays to an employee in any one year. The tax is the same percentage rate for all covered employers. It was initially levied primarily to finance the administration of unemployment compensation, and unemployment compensation administration continues to take a larger fraction of the budget of the Bureau of Employment Security than do the activities of the Employment Service.

The financing of the manpower program should be reexamined in the light of benefit-cost analysis. Its current financial arrangements have but a tenuous relationship to the whole package of manpower services that the Employment Service should provide. The tax itself is regressive in its effect. In view of the benefits the Employment Service affords to hard-to-place workers and the national interests served by a manpower program, there are good grounds for financing part of the cost from general tax funds of the Federal Government. In fact, a case can be made for financing the Employment Service by an equal sharing of the costs among employers, workers, and the government.

Benefit-costs analysis is particularly suited for decisions with respect to training and sheltered-work

programs and the encouragement of geographic mobility. The benefit aspects of training have been
briefly discussed. The costs, of course, vary with such
factors as the length of training, the level of occupational skill imparted, the facilities used, the training
allowances paid, and the sponsoring agency. For example, the training costs per trainee on 790 projects
under the Manpower Development and Training program were $313 for clerk-typist, $867 for auto mechanic, $1,106 for licensed practical nurse, and $1,218
for computer programmer.[14] In addition there were
the costs of government allowances to trainees for
living expenses during the training period. The actual total cost (training costs, allowances, administration, etc.) for institutional projects in 1963 averaged
$1,356 per trainee, with the cost for 15 per cent of
the trainees under $400 and for another 15 per cent
$2,500 or more.[15] These figures make no allowance
for opportunity costs—the earnings' losses of trainees
during training, which can be calculated from the
earnings of a comparable group of nontrainees.

The average cost for on-the-job training projects

[14] *Education and Training, the Bridge between Man and
His Work*, Third Annual Report of the Secretary of Health,
Education, and Welfare to the Congress on Training Activi-
ties under the Manpower Development and Training Act,
April 1, 1965, U.S. Government Printing Office, Washing-
ton, D.C., 1965, p. 15.

[15] *Manpower Research and Training under the Manpower
Development and Training Act of 1962, Report of the Secre-
tary of Labor*, U.S. Government Printing Office, Washington,
D.C., 1965, p. 11.

approved in 1964 was about $590 per trainee.[16] On-the-job training costs are low partly because most of the trainees are paid some wages by the sponsor during the training period and, therefore, are not granted allowances by the government.

Two benefit-cost studies of retraining programs for unemployed workers have concluded that the value of the training undoubtedly far exceeded its cost.[17] Even without allowance for any social or psychological gains, the expected benefits substantially outweigh the costs (including opportunity costs). One of the studies estimated that the increased earnings as a result of the training probably were sufficient to pay off total training costs in less than a year, but for females the pay-off period was about three times as long as for males.[18]

With more studies it should be possible to compare different types of training in terms of net gains and pay-off periods. Similar studies might be made for work-study projects under the Poverty Program, for sheltered workshops abroad, and for government subsidy programs to encourage geographic mobility. With a broader range of studies, it might be possible to compare the net gains from training with those estimated for still other types of manpower activity.

[16] *Ibid.*, p. 35.

[17] Somers and Stromsdorfer, "A Benefit-Cost Analysis of Manpower Retraining" (see n. 11); and Page, "Retraining under the Manpower Development Act: A Cost-Benefit Analysis" (see n. 11).

[18] Somers and Stromsdorfer, p. 181.

Social Values and National Interests

Benefit-costs analysis is not an answer machine. Rather it is a tool to aid in policy and budget decisions. An orderly framework is provided for tying specific benefits to specific costs and for informing policy-makers of the items and effects that need to be considered in policy formulation and revision. Obviously, benefit-cost analysis is most persuasive where cause-and-effect relationships are clear and the benefits and costs are measurable. Where the relationships are cloudy and the effects are diffuse and difficult to quantify, the guidance provided by benefit-cost analysis is less impressive.

In using benefit-cost analysis one must guard against depreciation or neglect of benefits that may be difficult to prove or to express in estimates. That is likely to happen where the benefits contain a large element of social value. In the end, governmental decisions are based on social and political as well as economic criteria. Training and other manpower programs may be justified on political and social grounds even when they may actually serve only to redistribute a given volume of unemployment and do not reduce total joblessness at all.

Manpower programs are likely to have important social benefits and significant elements of national interest. Social benefits include such items as elimination of discrimination in employment by race, sex, or age; assistance in rising out of a poverty status;

reduction in personal difficulties of social adjustment; and curtailment of crime and needs for welfare care. Work has a strong connection with personal attitudes and social adaptation.

Social welfare is also of national interest. That is the case, for example, in the current "War on Poverty." The Federal Government has an interest in the full development and effective utilization of the nation's human resources. That interest in human improvement is not only narrowly economic and military but also broadly political and cultural. The national government has a responsibility, for example, to help displaced farm families adjust to urban life or people in economically depressed areas move to expanding areas that offer more opportunities for an abundant life. In such changes, social and political adjustment can be as important to the nation as economic adjustment.

Recognition of the limitations of benefit-cost analysis and the importance of broad social and national interests should not, however, deter efforts to apply systematic reasoning to pressing issues in the manpower field. In the absence of a proper framework for thought, decisions tend to be made by hunch or compromise of personal views supported only by emotional and ideological appeals.

Clearly it is time to consider the adoption of the two main recommendations in this chapter. We need to reexamine the size and scope of the manpower program in the United States and the content of each of its functions in the light of benefit-cost analysis and of other systematic approaches. And we need to reexamine the financing of the Employment Service in the light of its changing role and of a benefit-cost analysis of its operations.

CHAPTER 8

The Contribution of Research

RESEARCH is the prime source of new, reliable knowledge, and such knowledge provides a basis for intelligent problem analysis, problem-solving, and rational judgments concerning policy issues. Benefit-cost analysis, of course, is based on research findings and, in turn, supplies leads and guidance for new research. An advantage of basic research is that it builds on the accumulation of tested knowledge and guides current research efforts into rewarding paths. Additive research not only enlarges previous findings but also serves to correct mistakes and to improve concepts and the structure of the basic theory.

Basic research in the manpower field involves informed analysis. Like basic research in other fields, it seeks out cause-and-effect relationships, and tries to find some unity in masses of fact. It uses many tools for discovering relationships and measuring them, for finding trends and patterns of work behavior, and for uncovering inconsistencies and logical shortcomings in generalizations about the world of work. The aim of manpower research is to distill the essential lessons from the variety of experience in this country and abroad.

Manpower research is a relatively new field. Much of its theoretical apparatus has been borrowed from the disciplines of economics, sociology, political science, and psychology. In that sense it is interdisciplinary. In addition, it is interdisciplinary because it deals with so many facets of human behavior. Each of the social science disciplines has a contribution to make to knowledge in the manpower field, and, in turn, the results of manpower research can aid in the more rounded development of knowledge and theory in those disciplines.

Because manpower research is still a relatively new and underdeveloped field, there is need to focus attention on promising approaches to pressing problems. There is also need to consider thoughtfully the effective utilization of research results, the expansion of research resources, and the strategy the government should follow in promoting research in the manpower field. Those subjects will be treated in that order in this chapter.

Some Major Research Needs

The small volume of fundamental research in the manpower field means that many subjects badly need further exploration and penetrating analysis. Some areas that require special attention now that the Federal Government has "an active manpower policy" are discussed in this section.[1]

[1] For a discussion of the kinds of research needed by the Federal-State Employment Service, see William Haber and D. H. Kruger, *The Role of the United States Employment Service in a Changing Economy*, The W. E. Upjohn Institute for Employment Research, Kalamazoo, Mich., February 1964, pp. 119-121.

Much more "labor-market" research is needed before Employment Service operations and various manpower programs will be well grounded on a solid understanding of work attitudes, job requirements, and labor mobility. There is nothing more practical and important for orienting one's thinking in the manpower field than basic knowledge of the motives and values of different elements of the work force, of the hiring and promotion policies of employers, and of the relative importance of factors influencing labor mobility. Such knowledge is essential for developing mobility guidelines, for counseling to influence occupational choice, and for programs to overcome labor shortages.

Although many studies of unemployment have been made and masses of unemployment statistics are available, it is surprising how unsatisfactory the state of our knowledge about joblessness is. Much more needs to be known about the effects of unemployment on morale, job search, and labor mobility and about the effects of various kinds of training, wage structures, and technological change upon the volume and character of unemployment. The hard-core or very long-term jobless are only imperfectly understood. Experimental and demonstration projects under the Manpower Development and Training program offer promise of significant insights into the hard-core problem and paths to effective remedial action.

The statistical underpinnings of manpower research have some weaknesses. The Census occupational categories used for the collection and presentation of manpower statistics should be thoroughly re-examined. They restrict analytical progress in certain directions. Classification by skill groupings and by groups of related skills would provide more meaningful aggregates of employer requirements. Aggregates so constructed would be more useful for education and training programs and for such other purposes as vocational counseling, the determination of company employment policies, and programs for improving labor mobility. Incidentally, some consolidation of requests for labor statistics from employers and a clear indication that all parts of the data collected are really useful would improve the Department of Labor's relations with business management.

The transition of youth from school to a career in the world of work needs a great deal of study. As was indicated in Chapter 6, that transition generally is much more successful in European countries, and we should learn why that is so. Comparatively little systematic knowledge exists concerning the role that different factors play in career choices and the ways by which youths qualify for various jobs. This country lacks detailed statistics on the entrance of youths into their first regular full-time employment. Great Britain collects such data from the National Insurance cards and publishes the statistics annually. The statistics are broken down by age, sex, industry entered, and type of occupation, including apprenticeship to a skilled craft, employment leading to a recognized profession, and other employment with a year or more of training. It is interesting to note that about half the boys in Britain entering employment at ages 15, 16, and 17 take jobs that carry with them at least a year of training. Similar data should be developed for the United States, perhaps by the Federal Old-Age, Survivors', and Disability Insurance system.

The experience of foreign countries with manpower planning can be very instructive. Experiments with programs and policies in different nations provide some testing of their relative effectiveness. Careful study of programs in European countries, such as sheltered workshops or subsidies for geographic mobility of workers, would enable us to learn from their experience, both favorable and unfavorable. At the same time, such research, permitting comparisons of labor-market behavior under different conditions, could broaden our knowledge of worker motivation and labor mobility.

Research in the training area in this country is just beginning to dig beneath the surface. That is true for vocational training in the schools as well as retraining of jobless adult workers. Even so, in the 1960's more research in the training area has been conducted in the United States than in all of Western Europe.[2] Actually, European countries have been noticeably deficient in manpower research.

[2] See Margaret S. Gordon, *Retraining and Labor Market Adjustment in Western Europe*, Office of Manpower, Automation, and Training, U.S. Department of Labor, 1965, p. 116. Incidentally this book is a good example of a valuable comparative analysis of foreign experience in one subject area, namely training.

CONTRIBUTION OF RESEARCH

Studies need to be made of the consequences of various types of training over a period of a decade or more. Some evidence seems to indicate that the non-instructional aspects of a training program, such as the screening for trainee selection, the training discipline, the program's stimulation to morale and aspiration, and the chance to make a good record, may help as much to improve the person's subsequent employment opportunities as the particular skills he learns in training. The extent to which that is true under various conditions should be thoroughly explored.

So far, benefit-cost analysis in the manpower field has been applied mostly to training. It should now be applied to other manpower activities. As explained in the previous chapter, such research promises significant long-term gains.

The subjects discussed above are only some of the top items on an agenda for manpower research. The needs are so great that research resources should be focussed as much as possible on projects that promise to be highly productive in terms of valuable results. The benefit-cost approach should also be applied to research itself.

Effective Use of Research Results

The importance of effective distribution and use of manpower information in an economy based on decentralized decision-making has been repeatedly stressed. In such an economy, the findings of manpower research need to be rapidly made a part of the mainstream of thought in industry and in government throughout the country. Since so much of our manpower knowledge is applied at the local level, efforts to spread research findings widely and to indicate the full range of their application in the community is much more important in the manpower field than, say, in the fields of national income analysis and policy or monetary research and monetary policy.

There are various ways of promoting the effective dissemination and utilization of the results of manpower research. One way is to package the information separately and specifically for different groups of users—workers, employers, counselors and job-exchange personnel, other public officials, and researchers. Another way is to explain, in releasing the results, how different users can apply them and what difference they make to particular groups. A third way is periodically to summarize and synthesize the results of a number of research projects in a particular field. That was competently done by Herbert S. Parnes in 1954 for the labor mobility field.[3] His report also served as a guide for future research. Summaries and abstracts designed for specific audiences are not, of course, substitutes for a full report on each research project, particularly for scholarly purposes.

Research personnel need to study the best ways to achieve proper distribution and use of manpower

[3] See H. S. Parnes, *Research on Labor Mobility*, Social Science Research Council, New York, 1954.

research findings. Clearly one aim should be to ensure rapid communication of, and response to, findings that point to adjustment in actual operations, in legislation, or in projected research.

Some research may be so abstract and esoteric that it seems to have little direct application to the world of affairs. That may not be the case, however, if others can develop the practical applications somewhat as engineers do with the findings of science. In any case, questions about the relative value of highly abstract research and the need for early results should not result in lack of care in research methodology or in failure to encourage the development of new and imaginative research techniques or ways of attacking manpower problems.

The Federal Government needs additional experienced researchers in the Office of Manpower, Automation, and Training, and it needs a panel of experts and individual consultants on whom it can call for advice on research matters and project improvement and evaluation. Encouragement of new research approaches and the use of outside experts for aid in the allocation of Federal support for manpower research will serve to draw more talent, especially young Ph.D.'s, into the manpower field.

With respect to local application of research findings and even the development of insights and research leads growing out of experience, persons trained in two or more of the social sciences for careers in government have proved quite effective in some cases. That, for example, has been true of two-year graduate students with master's degrees from the Woodrow Wilson School at Princeton University, who have worked in the programs of New Haven's Community Progress, Inc.

Furthermore, well-designed programs of project evaluation and experimental and demonstration projects can provide a considerable amount of new knowledge and some tentative conclusions. That is especially the case if some of the projects are planned in advance for the testing of hypotheses, and if arrangements for research are built into, say, a training project at the time it is approved.

Research Resources and Strategy

Increased resources need to be devoted to manpower research and manpower research administration in this country. Not only should the amount of research be considerably enlarged but the training of new recruits for research also needs to be expanded. Manpower research has tended to suffer from lack of a sufficient number of technically trained and imaginative persons in government to promote needed research, to allocate available research funds most effectively, and to develop ideas for the annual *Manpower Report of the President*. That document should set forth clearly an integrated conception of the major manpower problems facing the nation and a coordinated program for solving them. The Manpower Report should be sufficiently exciting intellectually to help attract young people of high talent into the manpower field.

Improvement in the manpower program, including its administration, depends in no small measure on a larger amount of research and a larger number of research-trained personnel. So far, Federal funds for research purposes under the Manpower Development and Training Act have been quite small. A total of $1 million was available in fiscal year 1963 for contract research outside the Federal government. In both fiscal 1964 and fiscal 1965 the total for such contract research was $2.1 million. For fiscal 1966, a sum of $3.8 million has been appropriated for external research contracts and grants, including the possibility of supporting a Ph.D. thesis as research. Actually, for the manpower program as a whole, research expenditures, strictly defined, have been under one per cent of total expenditures.

The distribution of available research funds for manpower and vocational education has been somewhat unbalanced. Under the Vocational Education Act of 1963, 10 per cent of all funds are reserved for various kinds of research including experimentation and evaluation. In fiscal year 1965-66 the research funds available for vocational education research in the Department of Health, Education, and Welfare exceeded $11 million, compared with around $6 million for manpower research available to the Office of Manpower, Automation, and Training in the Department of Labor for both in-house and outside research projects and administration. Although there has been coordination of research administration between the two departments, some projects (and researchers) that should more properly fall under the Department of Labor's manpower program are under the vocational education research program of Health, Education, and Welfare where the available funds are more ample.

In view of the nation's needs for firm and tested knowledge in various sections of the manpower field, the research budget of the Office of Manpower, Automation, and Training ought to be about $10 million for fiscal year 1966-67 and, say, $20 million by 1968-69. Such sums are, of course, but a drop in the bucket compared with Federal support for scientific research and development.

With Federal funds appropriated for research and research training in the manpower field likely to be strictly limited in the next few years, the Federal Government must use each dollar as effectively as possible. Some of the money needs to be used as seed investment or as leverage to move the existing research resources of universities, government, and private organizations more fully into manpower research. At first, the point of view of the Office of Manpower, Automation, and Training on the use of research funds was, in the main, rather short run. As the manpower program has been extended, however, the research horizon of the Administration has lengthened. Correctly, that has meant more stress on fundamental research and on continuing research programs.

A Federal program of support for manpower research and training of researchers should be based on a survey and analysis of the whole field. Such an analysis should take account of the national interest in manpower research, of the research that has been accomplished and will continue without Federal support, and of the areas and methods of research that promise the largest pay-off in terms of the needs of the Federal manpower program. That is a tall order.

Clearly the Federal Government needs a strategy for its program of support for manpower research. First, the manpower field should be carefully analyzed, and a set of research goals and high-priority projects should be selected on benefit-cost principles. They would serve as a guide in the allocation of research grants and contracts. Next, support for the training of new researchers should be closely joined with on-going manpower research, whether supported by the government or independently financed.

The spirit and methods of research are learned, mostly in universities, by communication and association with persons studying and conducting research. A final test of the student's research competence generally is the completion of a piece of research, usually in the form of a Ph.D. thesis, under the supervision of one or more professors. Federal aid to encourage more training in manpower research can, therefore, best be applied in the form of financial support to individuals during the period of their work on the thesis. That would mean direct encouragement of research in the manpower field for the graduate student's first major research project. Prior to that, most good graduate students have fellowship support supplied from a variety of sources.

In allocating its support for manpower research and research training, the Federal Government has to balance two needs. One is the need for the best possible research and the best possible training for research competence. The other need is to develop a respectable volume of research capability in areas of scarcity in manpower research, particularly in the South and in nonmetropolitan communities, some of which may be well suited for a badly needed study of rural manpower problems. The recommendations of the thirteen-man Subcommittee on Research of the National Manpower Advisory Committee on such policy questions can be helpful.

Consideration should be given to the possibility of tying in a regional center of manpower research and research training with regional facilities for mind-stretching training for top staff in the manpower organization, especially in the Employment Service (as explained in Chapter 4). Care would need to be taken to avoid spreading research resources too much into training, but a major center might well find advantages and economies from some joining of the two functions.

Federal support of manpower research and research training would carry no real threat to the independence that is vital for research. The resources devoted to labor research (heavily in the labor-relations area) are so large that $10 million or even $20 million a year of Federal funds for support of manpower research would not be a major factor in the total labor-research—graduate-training picture. Instead, the problem would be to attract researchers with good reputations into the manpower field or, in many cases, back into manpower research, which they cultivated in the late 1940's or early 1950's but later abandoned for seemingly more promising research pastures. Some return is a distinct possibility in view of the upsurge of interest in manpower policy and research brought about by the Manpower Development and Training Act, the President's annual Manpower Reports, and the growth of manpower planning and activities abroad.

Small research conferences on special topics such as the training and use of manpower in rural areas, or the relationships between wages and labor mobility, would serve to keep researchers up-to-date, to stimulate more, and more appropriate, research, and to attract researchers into the manpower field. Innovation in manpower research can also be stimulated by special efforts to attract the interest of more psychologists, political scientists, and sociologists. Political scientists can, for example, bring relevance and reality into research by analyses of conditions in a locality, including the distribution of political power, that contribute to success or failure of local manpower programs.

The Office of Manpower, Automation, and Training is beginning to develop an institutional grant program for the expansion of research and research training at existing college and university manpower research agencies and for the development of new programs or centers at institutions that now lack such research or training resources. The allocation of such program support needs to be well designed to obtain maximum results in terms of research and training in the immediate future and in long-run terms. Geographic distribution is especially important in a program that should have considerable emphasis on regional and municipal application of research results and training.

The discussion in this chapter has been too broad to highlight it in the form of one or two major recommendations. Much stress has been placed on more adequate research funds and their effective administration in a country that already has some thirty university research agencies in the labor relations and manpower fields. A good part of the strategy of the Federal Government should, therefore, aim at contributions to leadership and to coordination of manpower research and research training.

CHAPTER 9

....

Conclusion

....

WE LIVE in a job economy. Less than 15 per cent of the nation's work force are self-employed. The rest are jobholders and job-seekers. Paid employment supplies most of their income and occupies most of their days. Hence, preparing for work, securing employment, and moving up occupational ladders are matters of crucial importance to the American people.

Manpower planning seeks to improve the human resources of the country and to enlarge their work effectiveness over the long run. Thus it aims to raise the productivity of the economy. It is part of the nation's overhead investment in a worthwhile and creative life for the gainfully employed population.

Democratic Values and the Large View

In a free and democratic society, manpower responsibilities are widely diffused. Labor mobility is not centrally controlled. Workers and managements freely make their own decisions about employment, and enjoy or suffer the consequences.

What society through government can and does do is to lend a helping hand. It offers intelligent guidance and facilities to aid in the achievement of proper mobility of labor between occupations, areas, firms, and industries. The government's help should include the best available job information and expert assistance and advice in the matching of individuals and jobs. Employment analysis and the spread of knowledge about jobs expands the horizons of workers along with their occupational opportunities. Through a properly functioning system of public employment exchanges the freedom of the individual is enlarged.

Thus a well-conceived manpower program promotes the well-being of the individual and the individual firm. It affords support to democratic values. By assisting workers in self-development, manpower planning and programs enhance the dignity of the individual, enlarging his opportunity to shape his own work destiny.[1]

The helping hand of government needs to be guided by a broad, long-range view of manpower problems and their solutions. This "large" view necessarily means central use of foresight and over-all planning. Some general oversight is necessary to see that the nation's human resources are used effectively in the national interest. The national interest must be considered along with the interests of individuals, individual firms, and the locality. For the most part, compatibility and mutual support exist among all those interests. It is the national government's responsibility to provide manpower information, perspective, and leadership in promoting the goals of a free and democratic society.

[1] For an elaboration of this theme see Henry David, *Manpower Policies for a Democratic Society*, Columbia University Press, New York, 1965, especially pp. 9-14.

CONCLUSION

Reliance on persuasion to achieve manpower goals means that considerable attention must be devoted to the communication of the information and guidelines developed at the national level and to their application and administration at the local level. The balance between the central and local functions and responsibilities changes, of course, with developments in the economy and in our understanding of manpower problems.

Under manpower planning in a free and democratic society, shifts in function and responsibility between national and local levels occur in both directions. Manpower policies, because they bear so directly on the lives of individuals, must always be applied locally, and the quality of local application largely determines the success of the whole program.

It is with such considerations in mind that the manpower programs in the United States, Great Britain, West Germany, and Sweden were examined. That examination has led to a number of recommendations designed to improve manpower operations in the United States in line with the spirit of our democratic institutions. Stress has been placed on specific proposals that seem practical and highly desirable at this time. They do not, of course, constitute a complete manpower program.

Summary of Major Proposals

At the ends of Chapters 3 through 7, major recommendations that grew out of the discussion in those chapters were summarized. Those eleven recommendations, restated somewhat differently, are as follows:

1. A program of vocational instruction for school youngsters should be instituted as part of the regular curriculum in the high schools, preferably spread over three years, the instruction being supplied by school "career counselors" whose training and pay would be shared by the Employment Service and the school authorities as in Sweden.

2. A national clearing center should be established and operated by the U.S. Employment Service for the purpose of providing job-exchange service for relatively scarce, high-talent manpower that has a nationwide market, such as high-level managerial personnel, professional-school graduates, and college and university graduates generally.

3. The Employment Service, particularly at the Federal and State levels, should have its own tripartite boards (representing employers, labor, and government) that would have an important, direct role in policy determination and would provide channels of communication between client groups and the top Federal and State managers of the Service.

4. Resident training centers should be established and operated jointly by the Federal Government and the States in each region for the additional training and broadening of high-level personnel in the Service, such as top staff in State headquarters, in the regional offices, and in city offices.

5. Companies should reexamine their hiring standards in the light of new knowledge and conditions;

CONCLUSION

hopefully, some lengthening of the probationary period specified in collective agreements can be negotiated so that formal barriers may be lowered for certain groups of applicants who may have educational and other shortcomings that could be remedied.

6. The manpower program should include Federal support for sheltered workshops as a means of preparing seriously disadvantaged workers for commercial employment, and the manpower authorities should experiment with a program of job creation in the household services area.

7. The gap between employment (or demand) planning and manpower (or supply) planning in this country should be bridged more effectively at the Executive and Congressional levels, in part by giving the manpower authorities some role in demand creation.

8. The Federal Government should develop and use a set of mobility guidelines for operating purposes and to encourage informed movement of workers and discourage ill-advised moves, both geographically and occupationally.

9. The Federal-State program for education and training in preparation for work is currently too short run and parochial in its emphasis; the entire program should be reexamined from the point of view of national mobility requirements over the next decade.

10. The size of the nation's total manpower program and the role of each of the various functions should be reexamined in terms of current and prospective

needs and in the light of benefit-cost analysis and other systematic approaches to budget-making.

11. The financing of the Federal-State Employment Service should be reviewed in the light of its new role as a manpower agency and on the basis of an analysis of the various benefits it provides to workers, employers, and the government.

In addition to these eleven specific recommendations this book has urged that more stress be placed on knowledge-generating research and on the distribution of useful information about manpower needs and opportunities. Research is the source of valid new information and is basic to conceptions for guiding the whole program. However, it is by extensive communication of information that the essence of research findings and analysis is brought to the local level where practical application of that knowledge must take place. In the manpower field, information is the connecting link between improved understanding and rational action.

This book has set forth a pattern of thought and a program of action. The two should be inseparable. With enlightenment plus communication plus willpower, the desired results can be accomplished.

APPENDIX

....

Manpower Development and Training Act of 1962, as Amended[1] (42 U.S.C. 2571-2620)

....

AN ACT

Relating to manpower requirements, resources, development, and utilization, and for other purposes.

Be it enacted by the Senate and House of Representatives of the United States of America in Congress assembled, That this Act may be cited as the "Manpower Development and Training Act of 1962."

TITLE I—MANPOWER REQUIREMENTS, DEVELOPMENT, AND UTILIZATION

Statement of Findings and Purpose

SEC. 101. The Congress finds that there is critical need for more and better trained personnel in many vital occupational categories, including professional, scientific, technical, and apprenticeable categories; that even in periods of high unemployment, many employment opportunities remain unfilled because of the shortages of qualified personnel; and that it is in the national interest that current and prospective man-

[1] P.L. 87-415, Mar. 15, 1962, 76 Stat. 24-33, as amended by P.L. 87-729, Oct. 1, 1962, 76 Stat. 679; as amended by P.L. 88-214, Dec. 19, 1963, 77 Stat. 422; as amended by P.L. 89-15, Apr. 26, 1965, 79 Stat. 75.

power shortages be identified and that persons who can be qualified for these positions through education and training be sought out and trained as quickly as is reasonably possible, in order that the Nation may meet the staffing requirements of the struggle for freedom. The Congress further finds that the skills of many persons have been rendered obsolete by dislocations in the economy arising from automation or other technological developments, foreign competition, relocation of industry, shifts in market demands, and other changes in the structure of the economy; that Government leadership is necessary to insure that the benefits of automation do not become burdens of widespread unemployment; that the problem of assuring sufficient employment opportunities will be compounded by the extraordinarily rapid growth of the labor force in the next decade, particularly by the entrance of young people into the labor force, that improved planning and expanded efforts will be required to assure that men, women, and young people will be trained and available to meet shifting employment needs; that many persons now unemployed or underemployed, in order to become qualified for reemployment or full employment must be assisted in providing themselves with skills which are or will be in demand in the labor market; that the skills of many persons now employed are inadequate to enable them to make their maximum contribution to the Nation's economy; and that it is in the national interest that the opportunity to acquire new skills be afforded to these people with the least delay in order to alleviate the hardships of unemployment, reduce the costs of unemployment compensation and public assistance, and to increase the Nation's productivity and its capacity to meet the requirements of the space age. The Congress further finds that many professional employees who have become unemployed because of the specialized nature of their previous employment are in need of brief refresher or reorientation educational courses in order to become qualified for other employment in their professions, where such training would further the purposes of this Act. It is therefore the purpose of this Act to require the Federal Government to appraise the manpower requirements and resources of the Nation, and to develop and apply the information and methods needed to deal with the problems of unemployment resulting from automation and technological changes and other types of persistent unemployment.

Evaluation, Information, and Research

SEC. 102. To assist the Nation in accomplishing the objectives of technological progress while avoiding or minimizing individual hardship and widespread unemployment, the Secretary of Labor shall—

(1) evaluate the impact of, and benefits and problems created by automation, technological progress, and other changes in the structure of

production and demand on the use of the Nation's human resources; establish techniques and methods for detecting in advance the potential impact of such developments; develop solutions to these problems, and publish findings pertaining thereto;

(2) establish a program of factual studies of practices of employers and unions which tend to impede the mobility of workers or which facilitate mobility, including but not limited to early retirement and vesting provisions and practices under private compensation plans; the extension of health, welfare, and insurance benefits to laid-off workers; the operation of severance pay plans; and the use of extended leave plans for education and training purposes. A report on these studies shall be included as part of the Secretary's report required under section 107;

(3) appraise the adequacy of the Nation's manpower development efforts to meet foreseeable manpower needs and recommended needed adjustment, including methods for promoting the most effective occupational utilization of and providing useful work experience and training opportunities for untrained and inexperienced youth;

(4) promote, encourage, or directly engage in programs of information and communication concerning manpower requirements, development, and utilization, including prevention and amelioration of undesirable manpower effects from auto-

mation and other technological developments and improvement of the mobility of workers;

(5) arrange, through grants or contracts, for the conduct of such research and investigations as give promise of furthering the objectives of this Act; and

(6) establish a program of experimental, developmental, demonstration, and pilot projects, through grants to or contracts with public or private nonprofit organizations, or through contracts with other private organizations, for the purpose of improving techniques and demonstrating the effectiveness of specialized methods in meeting the manpower, employment, and training problems of worker groups such as the long-term unemployed, disadvantaged youth, displaced older workers, the handicapped, members of minority groups, and other similar groups. In carrying out this subsection the Secretary of Labor shall, where appropriate, consult with the Secretaries of Health, Education, and Welfare, and Commerce, and the Director of the Office of Economic Opportunity. Where programs under this paragraph require institutional training, appropriate arrangements for such training shall be agreed to by the Secretary of Labor and the Secretary of Health, Education, and Welfare. He shall also seek the advice of consultants with respect to the standards governing the adequacy and design of proposals, the ability of applicants, and the priority of projects in meeting the objectives of this Act.

APPENDIX

Job Development Programs

Sec. 103. The Secretary of Labor shall stimulate and assist, in cooperation with interested agencies both public and private, job development programs, through on-the-job training and other suitable methods, that will serve to expand employment by the filling of those service and related needs which are not now being met because of lack of trained workers or other reasons affecting employment or opportunities for employment.

Labor Mobility Demonstration Projects

Sec. 104. (a) During the period ending June 30, 1967, the Secretary of Labor shall develop and carry out, in a limited number of geographical areas, pilot projects designed to assess or demonstrate the effectiveness in reducing unemployment of programs to increase the mobility of unemployed workers by providing assistance to meet their relocation expenses. In carrying out such projects the Secretary may provide such assistance, in the form of grants or loans, or both, only to involuntarily unemployed individuals who cannot reasonably be expected to secure full-time employment in the community in which they reside, have bona fide offers of employment (other than temporary or seasonal employment), and are deemed qualified to perform the work for which they are being employed.

(b) Loans or grants provided under this section shall be subject to such terms and conditions as the

Secretary shall prescribe, with loans subject to the following limitations:

(1) there is reasonable assurance of repayment of the loan;

(2) the credit is not otherwise available on reasonable terms from private sources or other Federal, State, or local programs;

(3) the amount of the loan, together with other funds available, is adequate to assure achievement of the purposes for which the loan is made;

(4) the loan bears interest at a rate not less than (A) a rate determined by the Secretary of the Treasury, taking into consideration the average market yield on outstanding Treasury obligations of comparable maturity, plus (B) such additional charge, if any, toward covering other costs of the program as the Secretary may determine to be consistent with its purposes; and

(5) the loan is repayable within not more than ten years.

(c) Of the funds appropriated for a fiscal year to carry out this Act, not more than $5,000,000 may be used for the purposes of this section.

Trainee Placement Assistance Demonstration Projects

SEC. 105. During the period ending June 30, 1967, the Secretary of Labor shall develop and carry out experimental and demonstration projects to assist in the placement of persons seeking employment through a public employment office who have successfully completed or participated in a federally assisted or financed training, counseling, work training, or work experience program and who, after appropriate counseling, have been found by the Secretary to be qualified and suitable for the employment in question, but to whom employment is or may be denied for reasons other than ability to perform, including difficulty in securing bonds for indemnifying their employers against loss from the infidelity, dishonesty, or default of such persons. In carrying out these projects the Secretary may make payments to or contracts with employers or institutions authorized to indemnify employers against such losses. Of the funds appropriated for fiscal years ending June 30, 1966, and June 30, 1967, not more than $200,000, and $300,000, respectively, may be used for the purpose of carrying out this section.

Skill and Training Requirements

SEC. 106. The Secretary of Labor shall develop, compile, and make available, in such manner as he deems appropriate, information regarding skill requirements, occupational outlook, job opportunities, labor supply in various skills, and employment trends on a National, State, area, or other appropriate basis which shall be used in the educational, training, counseling, and placement activities performed under this Act.

APPENDIX

Manpower Report

Sec. 107. The Secretary of Labor shall make such reports and recommendations to the President as he deems appropriate pertaining to manpower requirements, resources, use, and training; and the President shall transmit to the Congress within sixty days after the beginning of each regular session (commencing with the year 1963) a report pertaining to manpower requirements, resources, utilization, and training.

Index

[223]